Hidden Ireland Photography

ISBN: 9798546467821
Imprint: Independently Published

Emmet Tobin © 2021

Contents

[1] Bunmahon Beach, Co. Waterford. Pictured are the cliffs on the East side of the beach. The beach runs for approx. 2.7km. Sand dunes are located to behind the beach. The River Mahon enters the bay in the background or the picture adjacent to the cliffs.

[2] The Copper Coast, County Waterford. Aptly named due to the minerals present in the cliffs along the coastline. Pictured from the sandy beach located at Boatstrand.

[3] Fasting Budda, a granite statue located in Victors Way, Co. Wicklow. Established in 1996, the garden contains 7 major and 37 minor black granite sculptures. The major sculptures represent 7 phase transitions of a (creative) life cycle.

[4] The Split man, Victors Way, the sculpture represents the mental state of the dysfunctional human.

[5] A yacht anchored close to Dunmore East, Co. Waterford. Dunmore East is popular with tourists for its quaint streets, picturesque beaches and coves for swimming.

[6] Thomas Maher, 20 O'Connell Street, Waterford. A historic bar and public house. Once reserved for gentlemen only. It now serves all equally and without prejudice

[7] J&K Walsh, a premises' that has reinvented itself over the decades. Originally a general store it is now a popular bar. Small in footprint but lots of character.

[8] Curraghmore House, Portlaw, Co. Waterford. home of the Marquis of Waterford and his ancestors since 1170, includes an arboretum, a bridge built in 1205 and a unique shell grotto built and decorated by the Countess of Tyrone in 1754.

[9] A sculpture located in the garden estate of Curraghmore, illustrates great detail by its creator. The estate has many sculptures in various materials such as wood, granite and limestone.

[10] Reginald's Tower, built by Vikings in 914 and re-built by the Anglo Normans in the 12th century with a further top two floors added in the 15th century. The tower is now managed by the Office of Public Works. Picture taken from across the Suir River in Ferrybank, North Waterford.

[11] Our Lady of Johns Park, a state of the Bless Mother adjacent to a home in the city of Waterford. Devotion to Our Lady is a pillar of the Catholic identity in Ireland.

[12] Saint Manchán's Well, County Offaly. Saint Manchán's feast day is celebrated on the twenty-fourth of January. The well is particularly deep and the water is pitch black because of the surrounding bog. The legend of the healing benefits of the water are just as powerful to this day. He died either in 661 (according to the annals of Clonmacnoise.

[13] Grazing Sheep, Comeragh Mountains. The Mountain range lies to the west of the County of Waterford.

[14] Saint Manchán's Well, footpath and entrance to the holy well.

[15] Mahon Falls – a view towards the sea from the Comeragh Mountains. The relatively flat farmland below leads into Dungarvan bay. Mahon falls is popular with hill walkers and hikers.

[16] A Bi-cycle is left against the gate leading to the ruined chapel of St. Mella's Kell, located near St Manchans well.

[17] Holy Water, the use of holy water in the Catholic tradition as a sacramental tool in prayer and blessing. Any plastic bottle (from milk or soft drink) can be used to bring holy water from the site to the home or distribute to friends and family.

[18] School House, an old school house with a typical design seen in the late 1800's into the 20th century. Many school houses throughout Ireland have been reimagined as domestic homes and converted to modern use.

[19] Peat Moss Collection, Ferbane, Co. Offaly, while mass produced briquettes of turf are a product of the midland bogs, peat moss is also harvested from the bogs and used as compost and plant food.

[20], [21] Stacked turf drying, the turf that is seen here has been "footed" without the use of machinery in what is a very physically demanding activity. Once cut and footed, the turf is stacked to allow it to dry naturally prior to storage for the winter and use in fireplaces throughout Ireland.

[22] Row after Row, footed turf is yet to be stacked.

[23] Madigans' Off license, a popular source of take away alcohol, famous for its large bottles of Guinness. A family owned and run business; it stands proud as one of the few remaining independent off licenses.

[24] Arriving home, a small fishing boat returns to the inner safety of Dunmore East Harbour, Co. Waterford

[25] Suir River pictured from the Old Kilmeaden area of Co. Waterford, the wide meandering river runs next to the Greenway and tourist railway track.

[26] Fishing Boats, boats moored in Dunmore east, Co. Waterford.

[27] Platform 03, Plunkett Train Station, names after one of the 1916 Easter Rising Irish mean killed by British forces. The station is severed by three platforms.

[28] The finger, the inscription on the fingertip reads- Create or die. Situated in Victors Way, Co. Wicklow.

[29] Journey Man, representing man stuck in an unending journey, the sculpture captures the struggles and effort of this tormented person.

[30] The Estuary, a merchant vessel heads seaward from the Port Of Waterford. The wide river can accommodate large merchant and passenger ships, boasting one of Europe's widest city based estuaries.

[31] BoatStrand, the small village located in Co. Waterford is a popular location for swimming and fishing.

[32] Dunmore East, a calm sea on a dull day, pictured is the lower strand

[33] Afloat, a small fishing boat prepares to land after a days fishing

[34] Anchored, a solitary boat is anchored along the copper coast

[35] Loftus Hall, pictured from across the bay from Dunmore East. Loftus hall is situated on the Hook peninsula in Co. Wexford. Legend has it that the premises is haunted to this day. Legend has it that during a storm a stranger approached the Hall on horseback after his ship was driven into nearby slade Harbour with rough seas. He was invited in to seek shelter and spent some days with the Tottenham Family who were living at the Hall at the time. One night during a card game, young Anne Tottenham dropped a card and upon bending down to retrieve it, she noticed that this dark stranger had cloven hoofs instead of feet. As soon as he realised what she had seen, he shot through the roof in a ball of flames.

[36] Guillamene Swimming Cove, once reserved for gentlemen only, this sign is located in the Newtown area of Tramore.

[37] Ferrybank, a engine steams towards Waterford city from the Wexford direction

[38] Cape Clear, the pier in the North Harbour, Cape Clear is Irelands most southerly point.

[39] Bargareth, a familiar sight in Waterford Port, maintained and operated by fastnet shipping.

[40] Dún Aonghasa, Arran Island, (Co. Galway), spectacular cliff overlooking the Atlantic Ocean, the fort is about 900 metres from the visitor centre and offers views of up to 75 miles of Irish coastline

[41] Shop Bar, a once common site in public houses throughout ireland. The front of the premises served as a shop and hardware store stocking the basics. With the bar situated through a partition.

[42] Dromana Gate is a Hindu Gothic gate dating from around 1830, The only one of its kind in Ireland.

The gate was originally built from wood and papier mache to greet the owner of the Dromana Estate, Henry Villiers-Stuart and his wife, Theresia Pauline Ott of Vienna, on returning from their honeymoon in 1826. The couple were so enchanted with the gate it was reconstructed in stone in later years.

[42] Doneraile, Tramore, Co. Waterford, with viewed ofTramore Bay, the Sandhills and Brownstown Head at the opposite side of the Bay. It is named after a local landlord, Lord Doneraile, who donated the land to the Townspeople. On the walk with its wide open spaces you will pass a monument dedicated to one of the worst shipwrecks that Tramore Bay has ever seen – the loss of the British "Sea Horse" in January 1816.

[1]

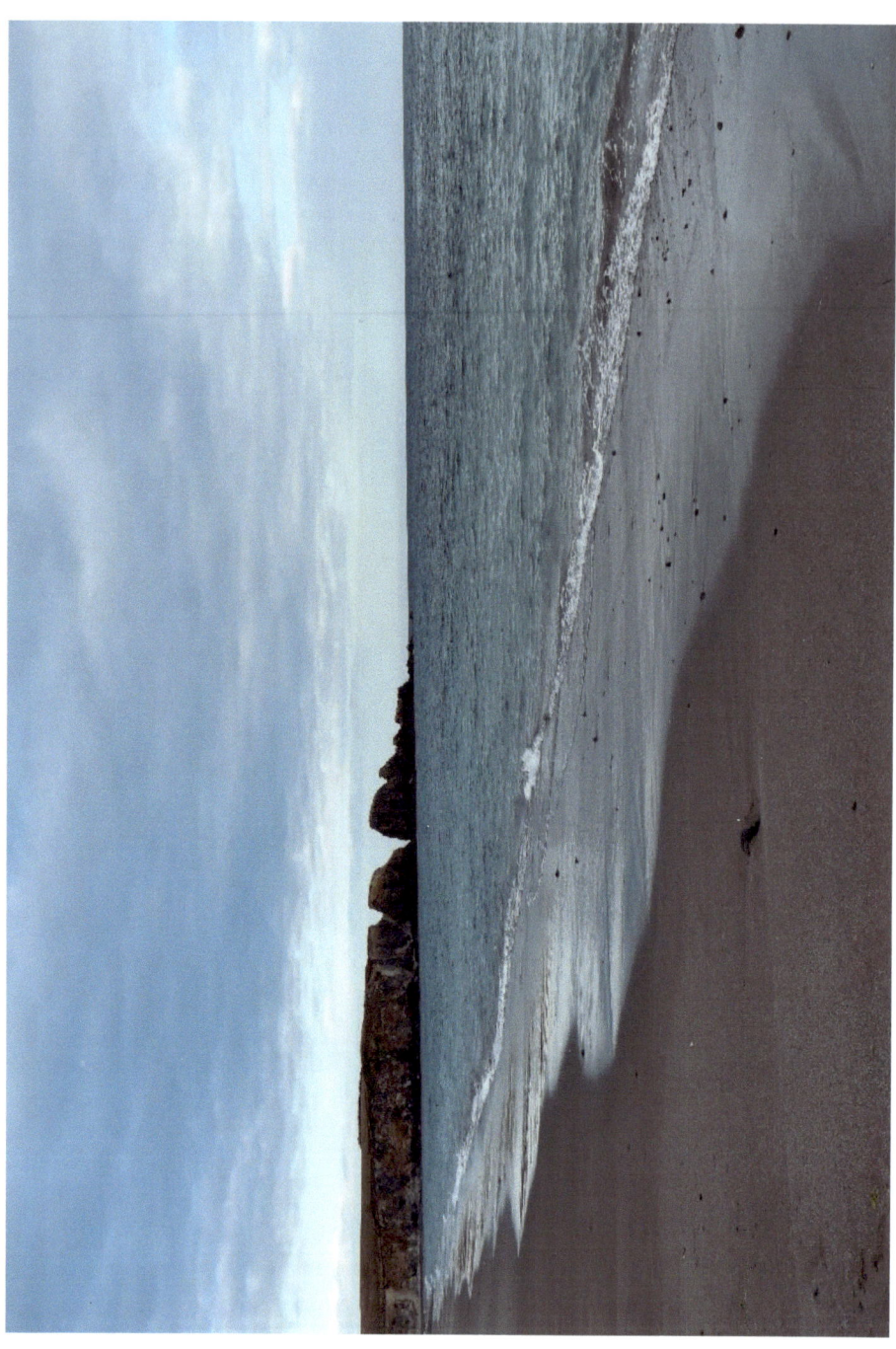

[2]

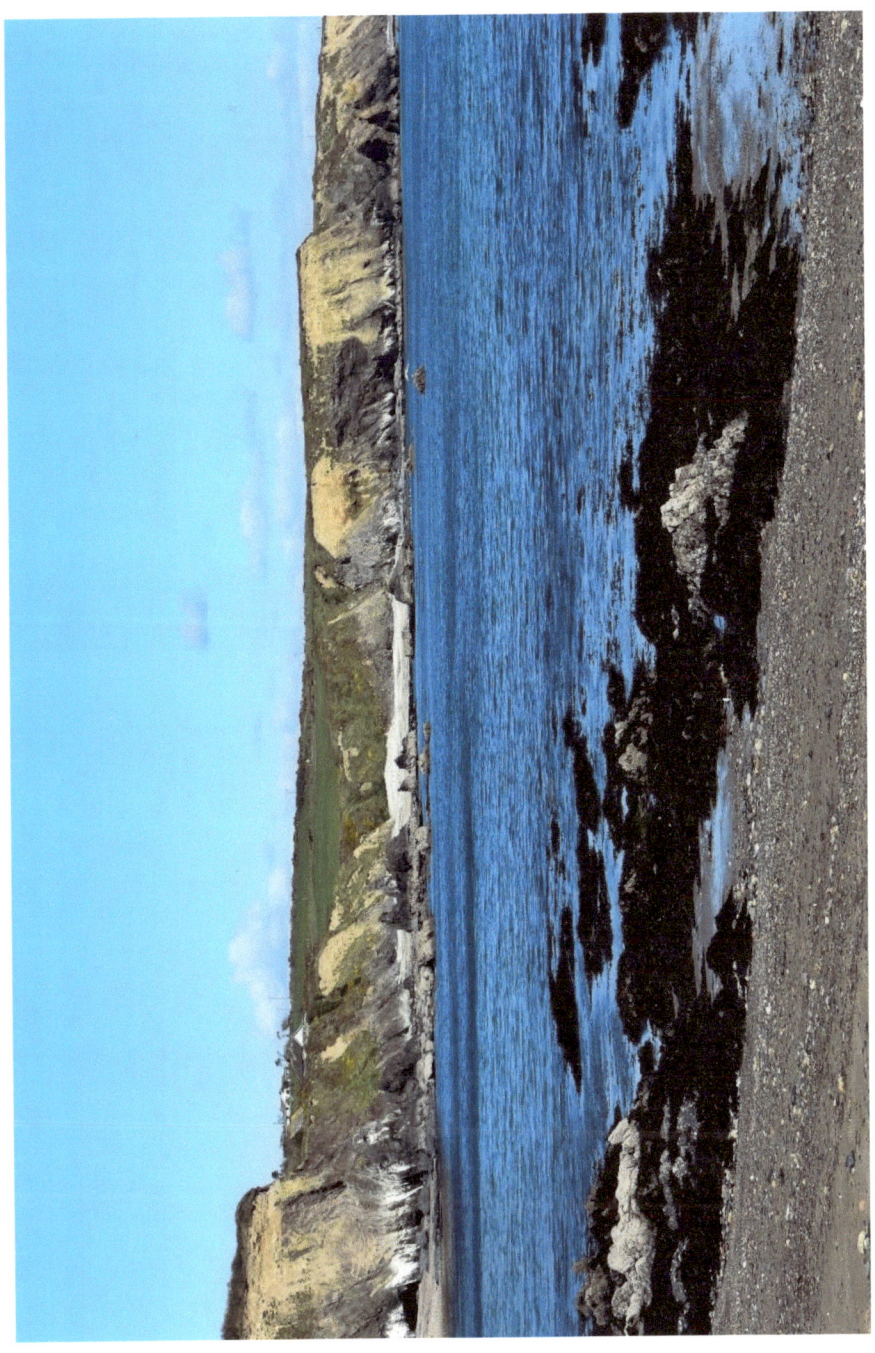

[3]

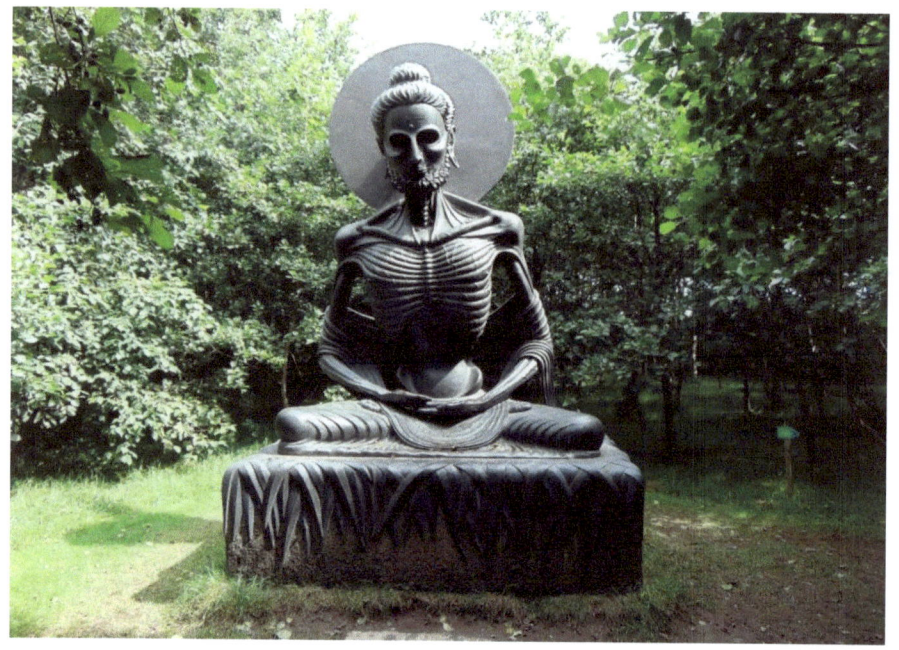

[4]

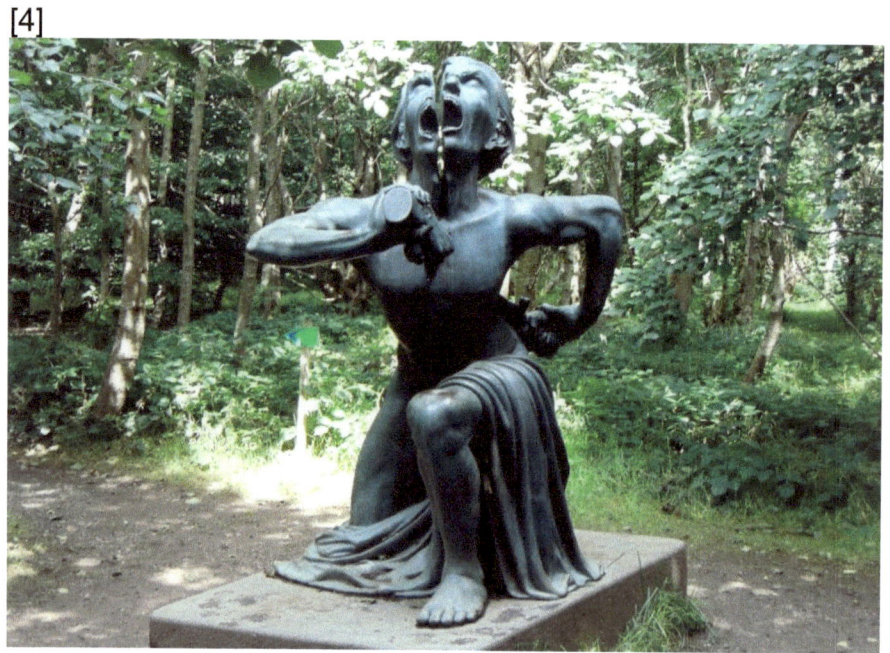

[5]

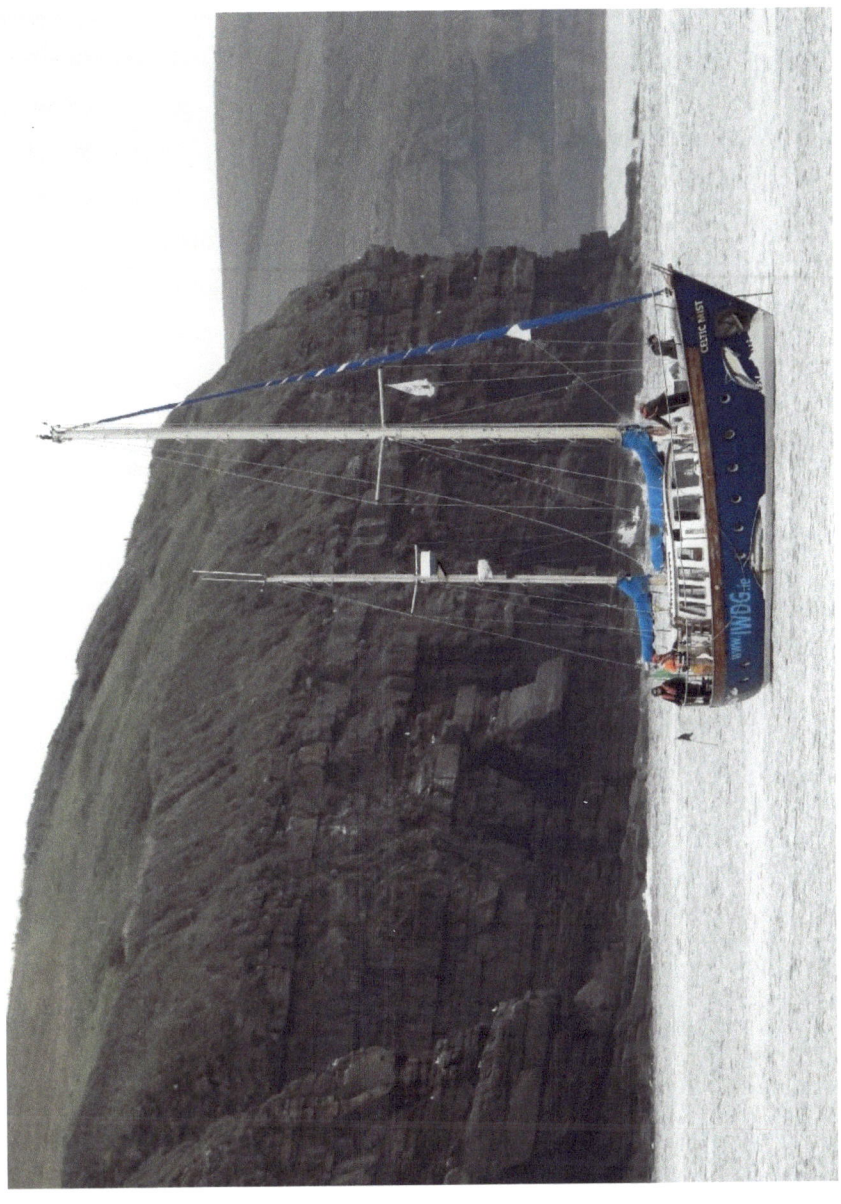

[6]

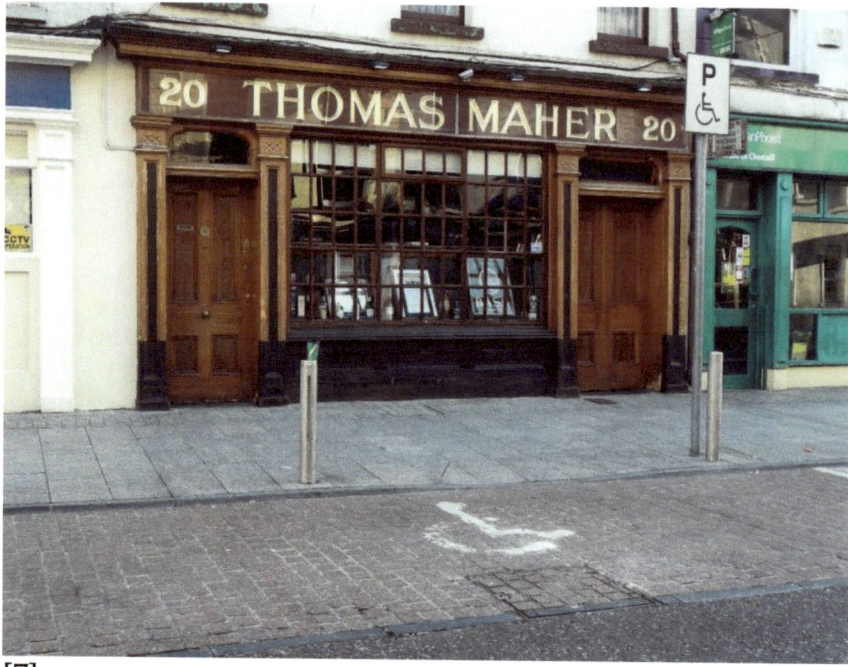

[7]

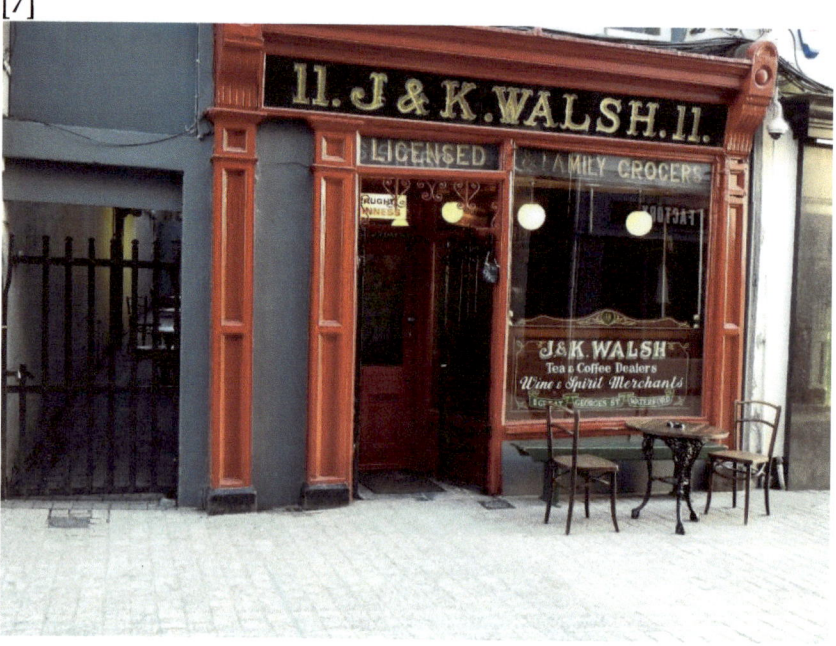

[8]

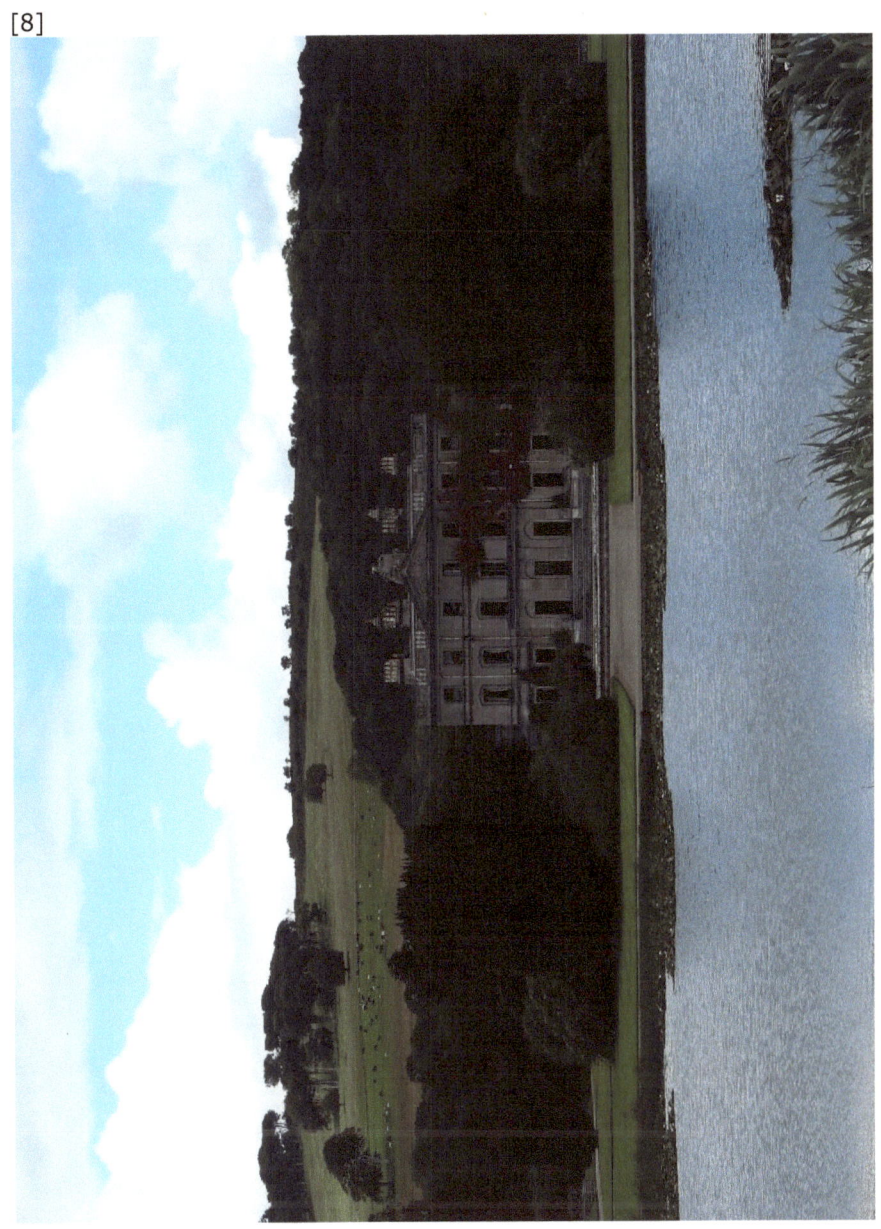

[9]

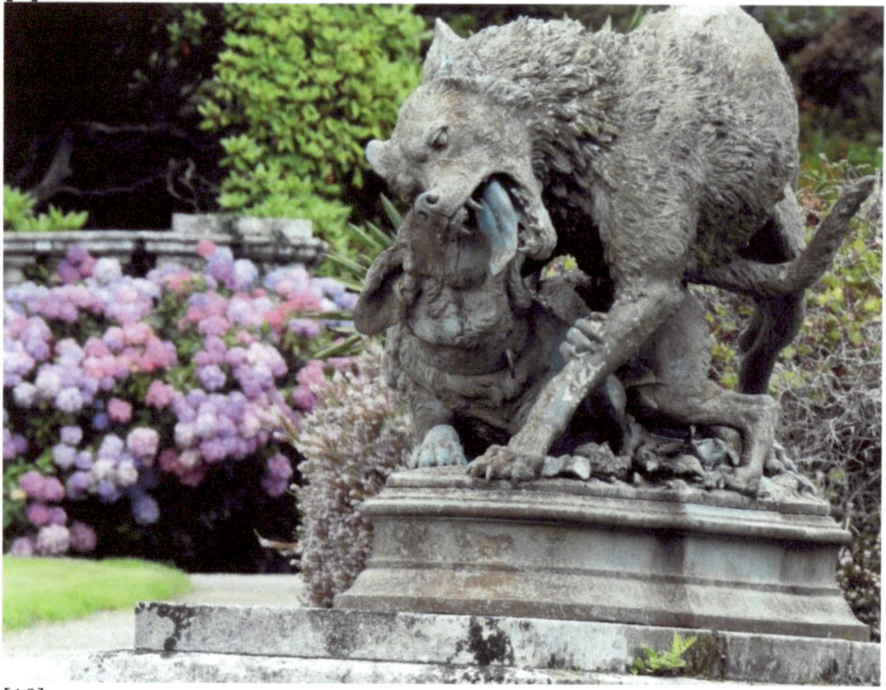

[10]

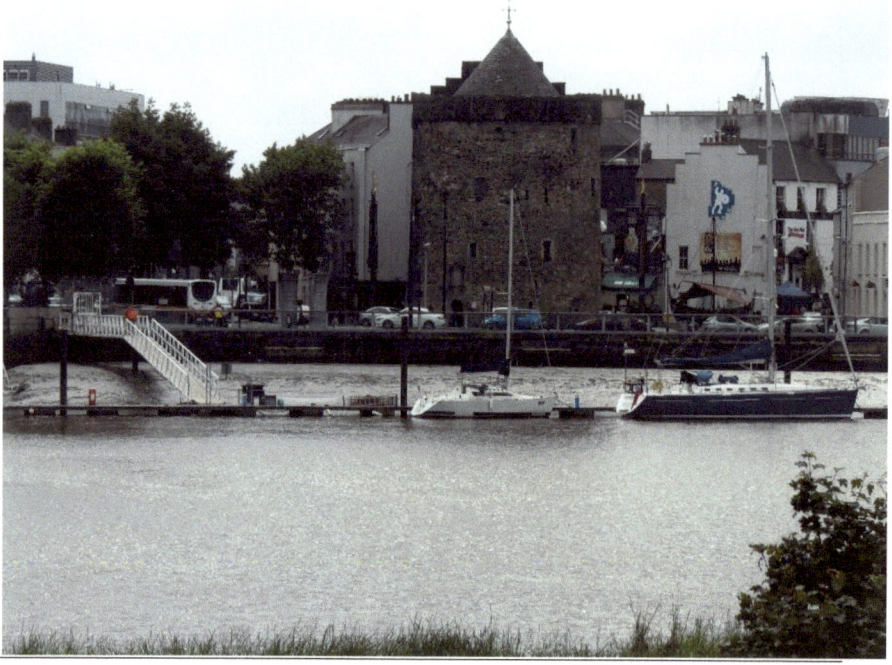

[11]

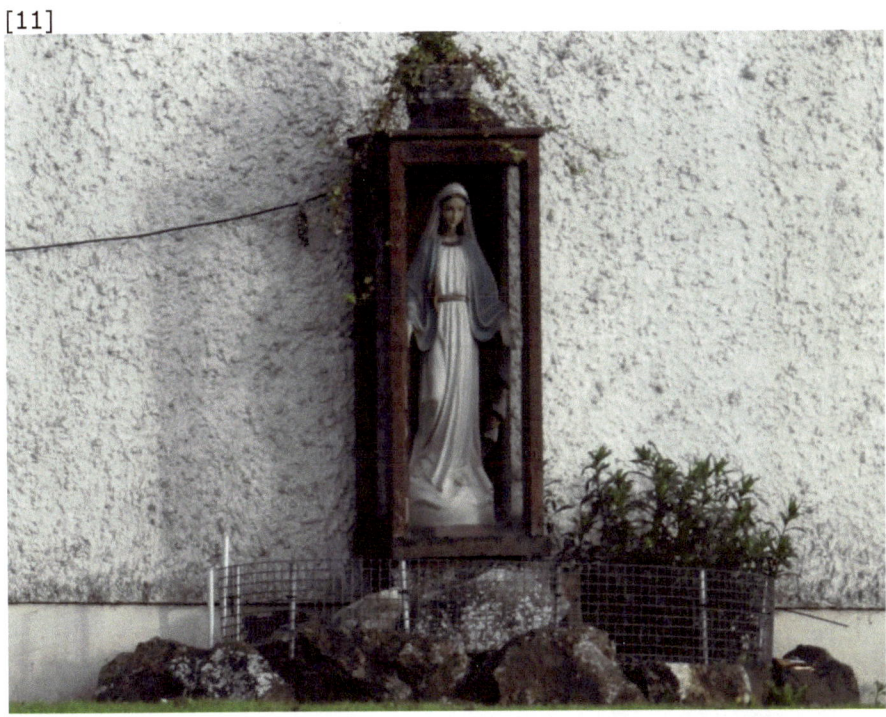

[12]

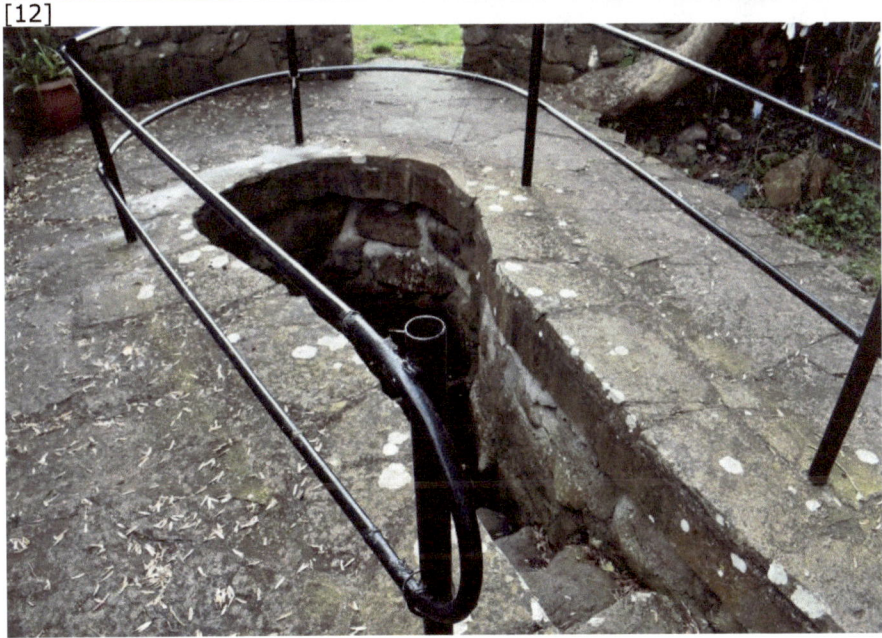

[13]

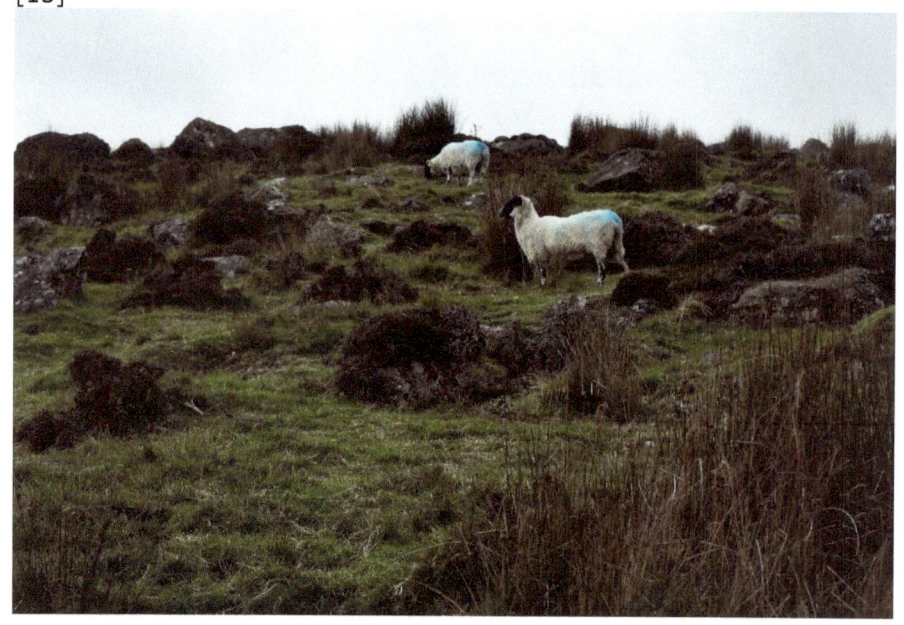

[14]

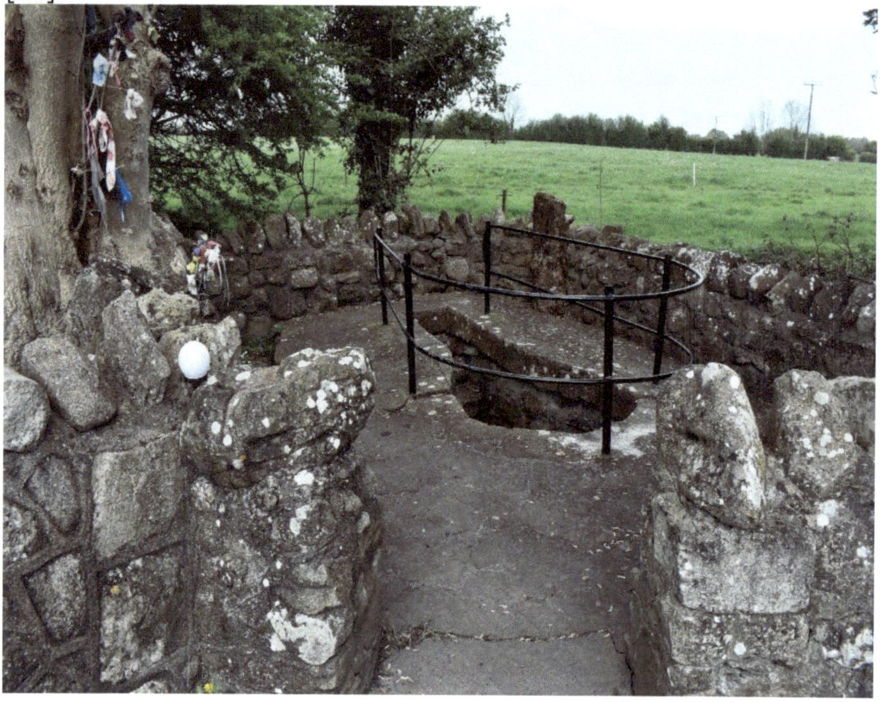

[15]

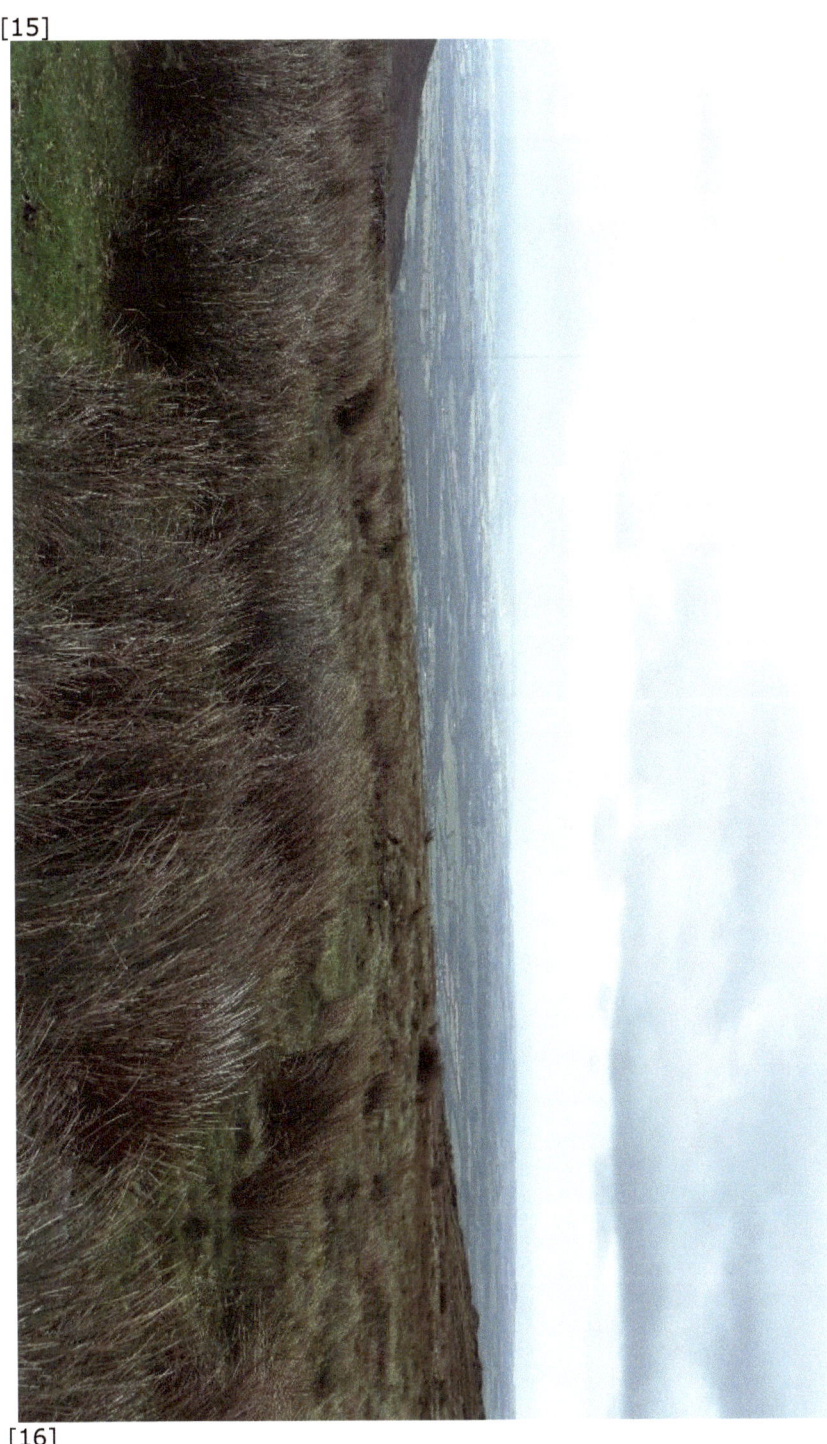

[16]

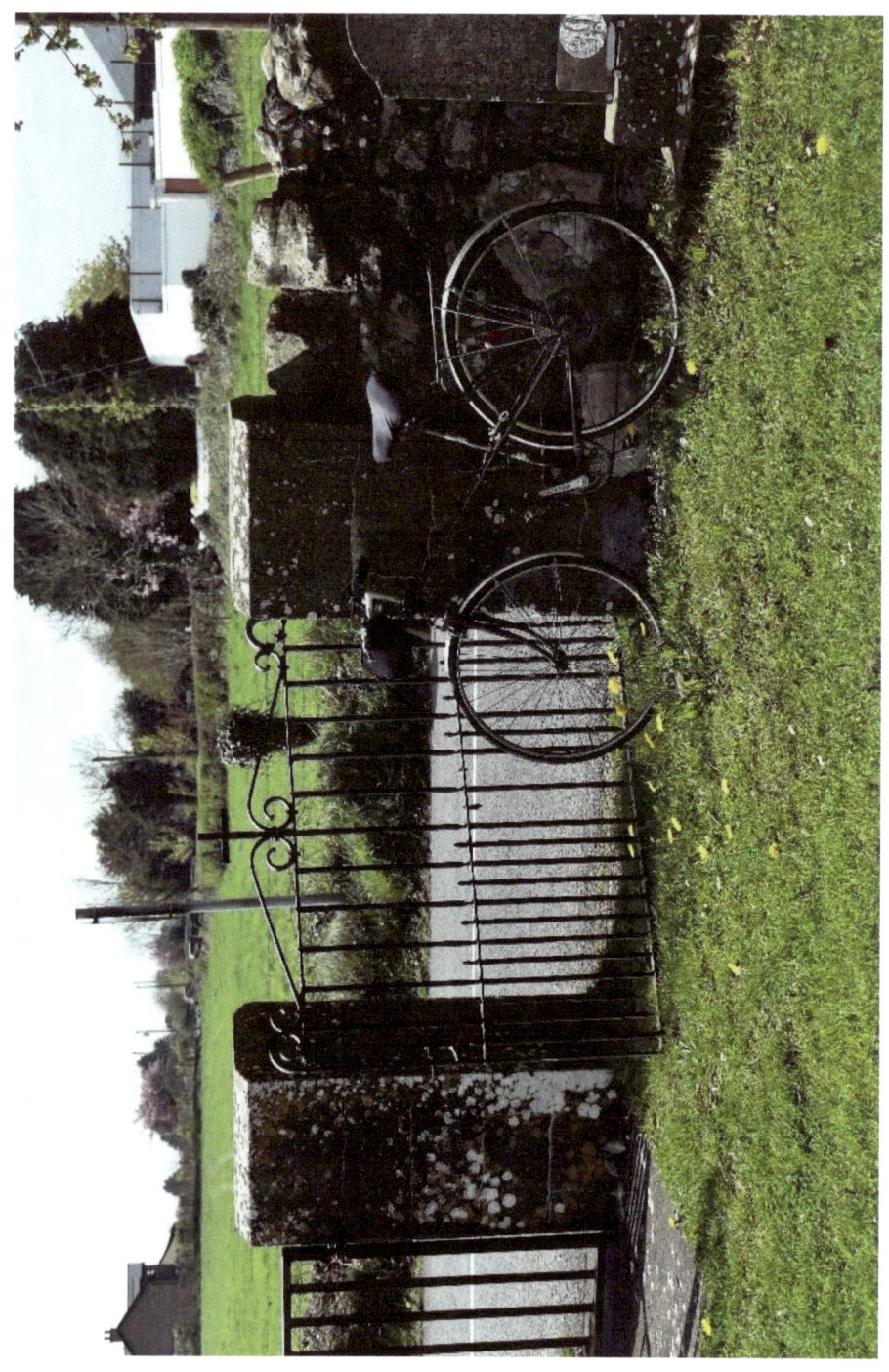

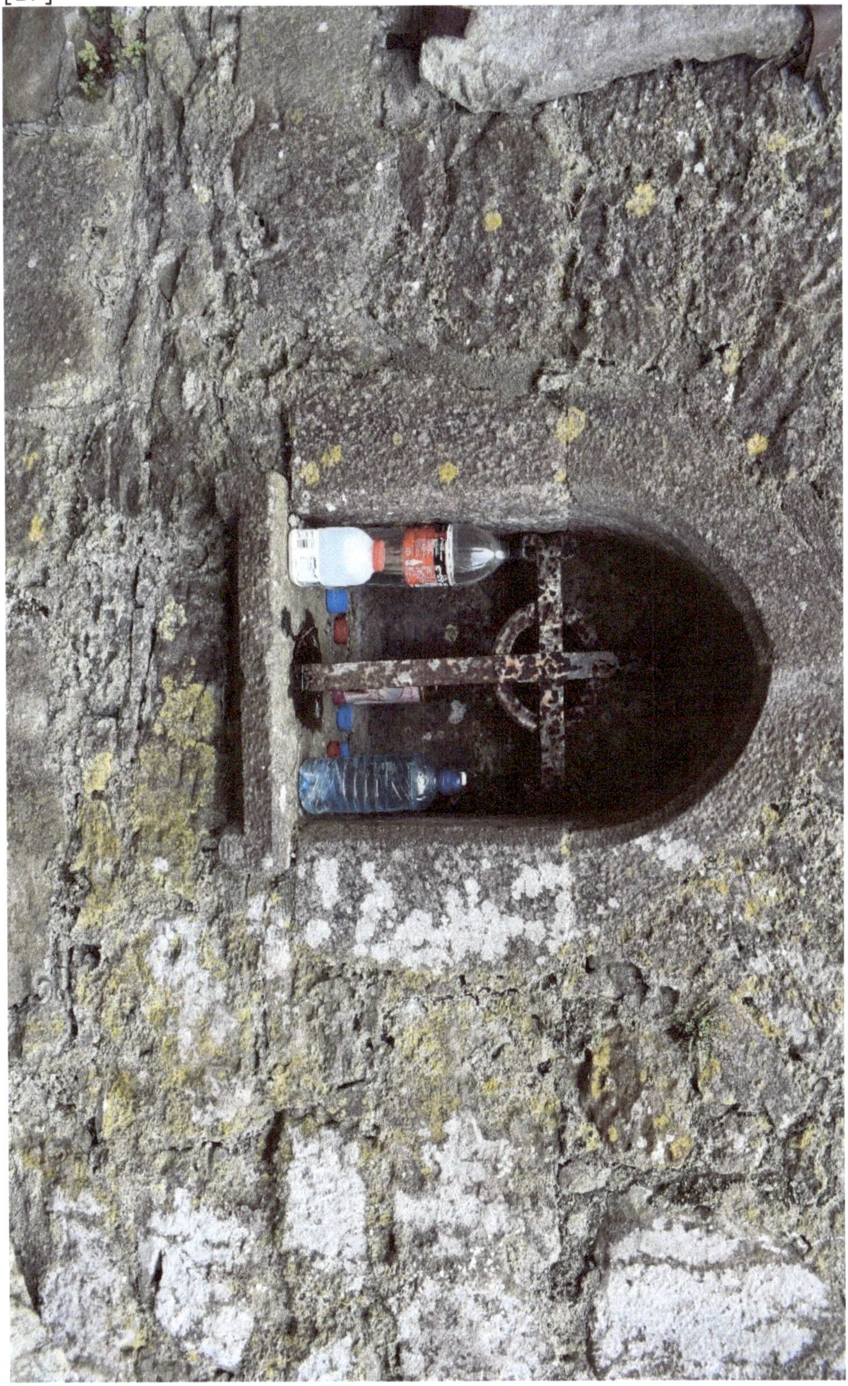

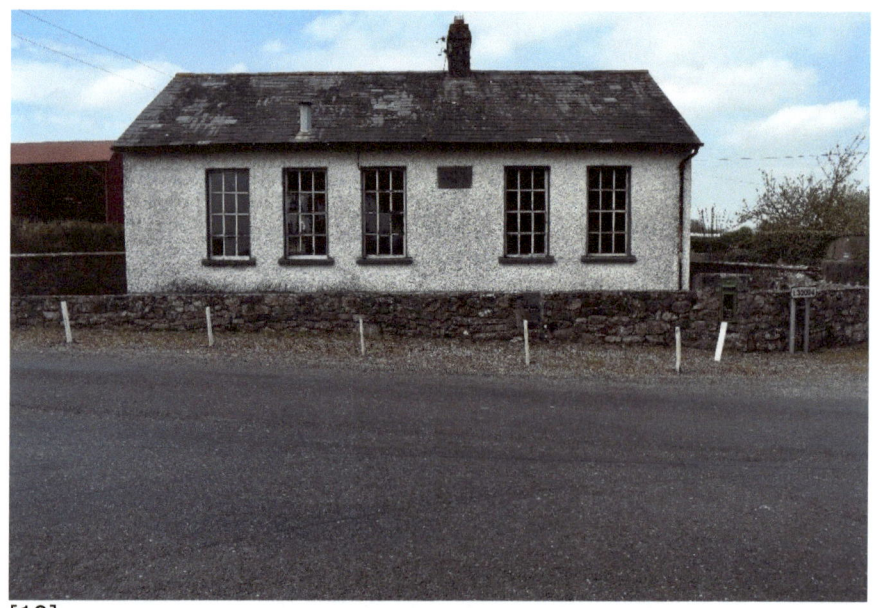
[19]

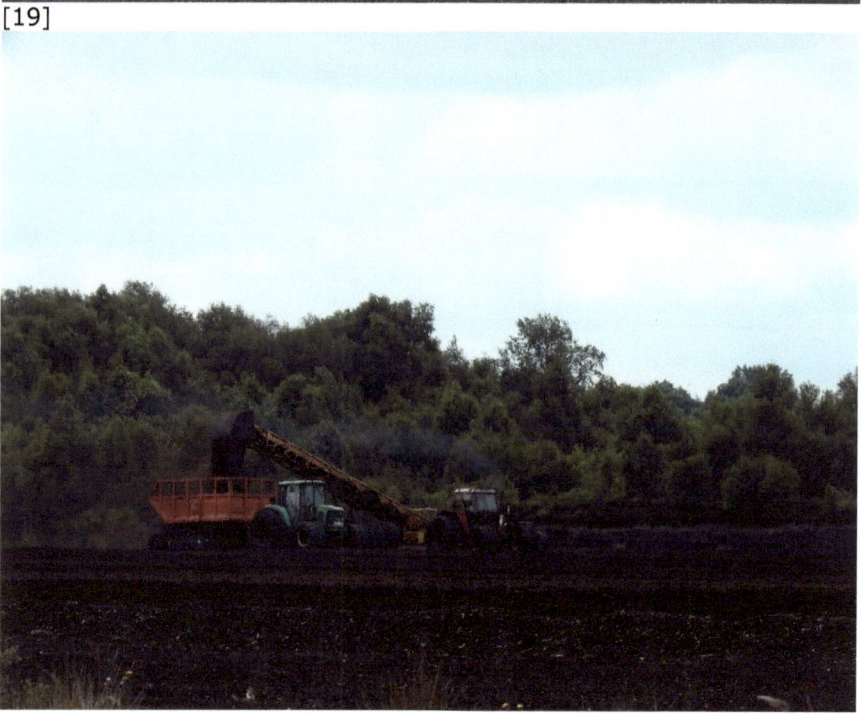

[20]
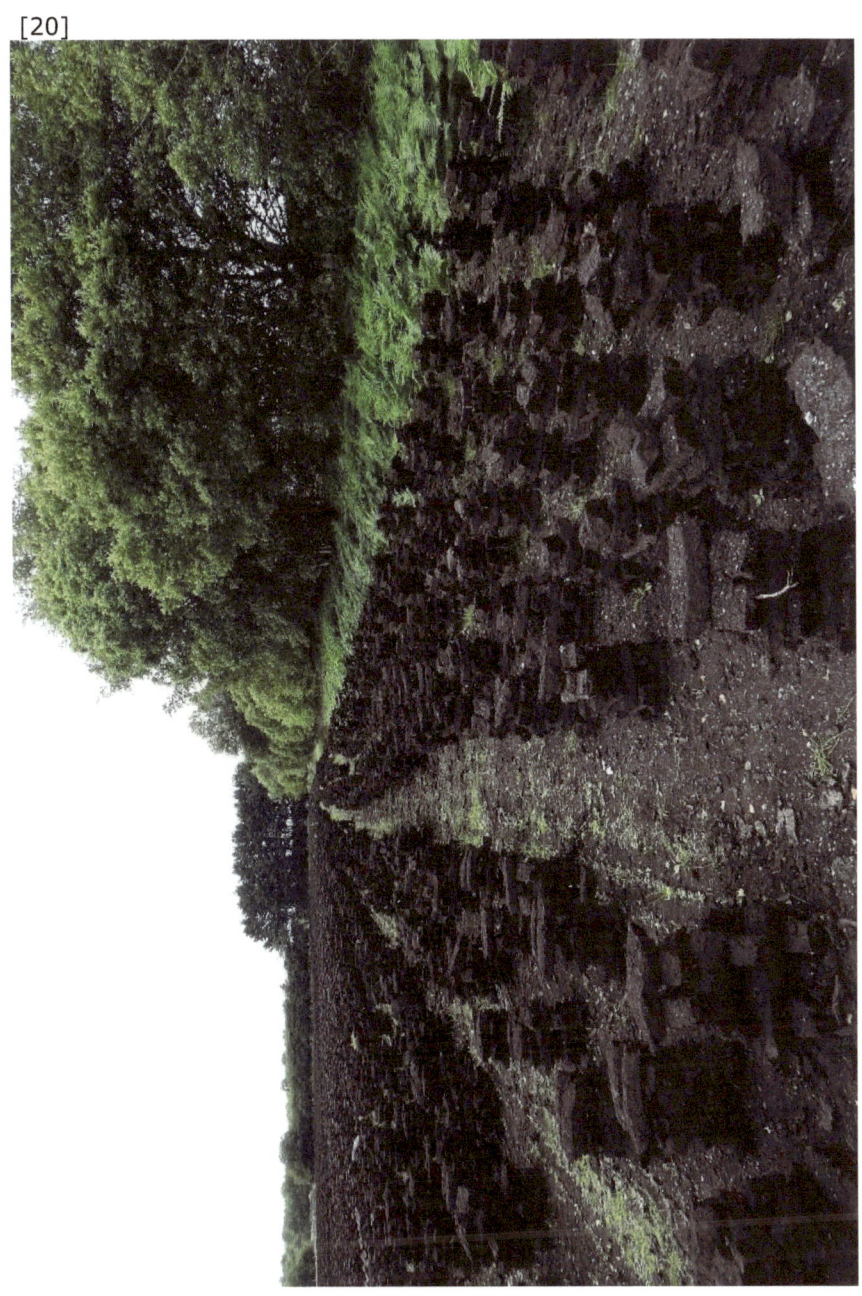

[21] Stacked turf

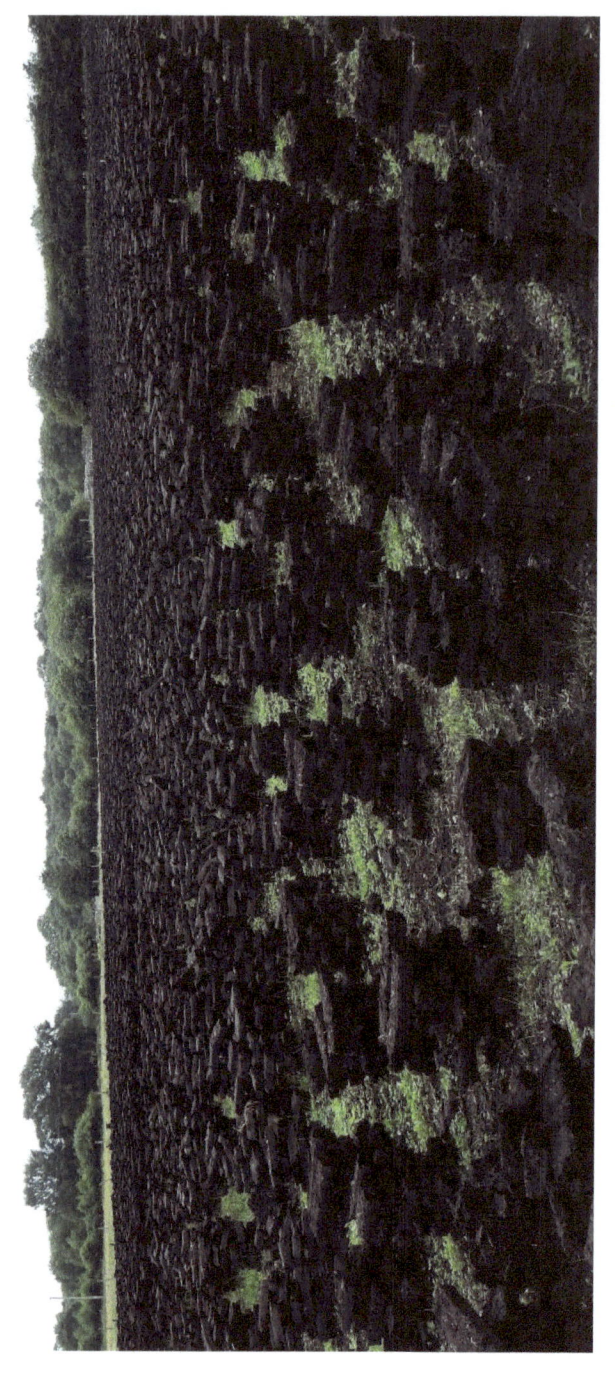

[22]

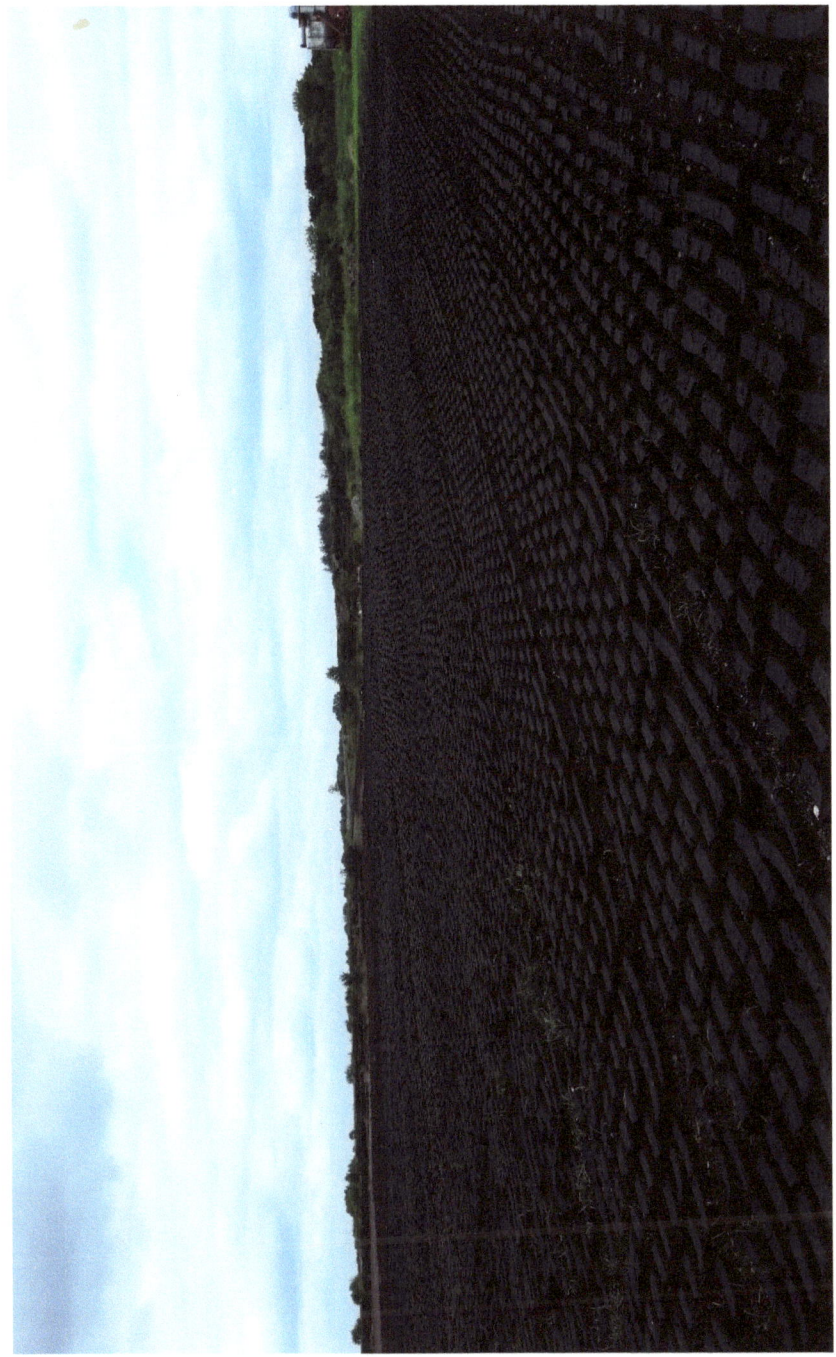

[23]

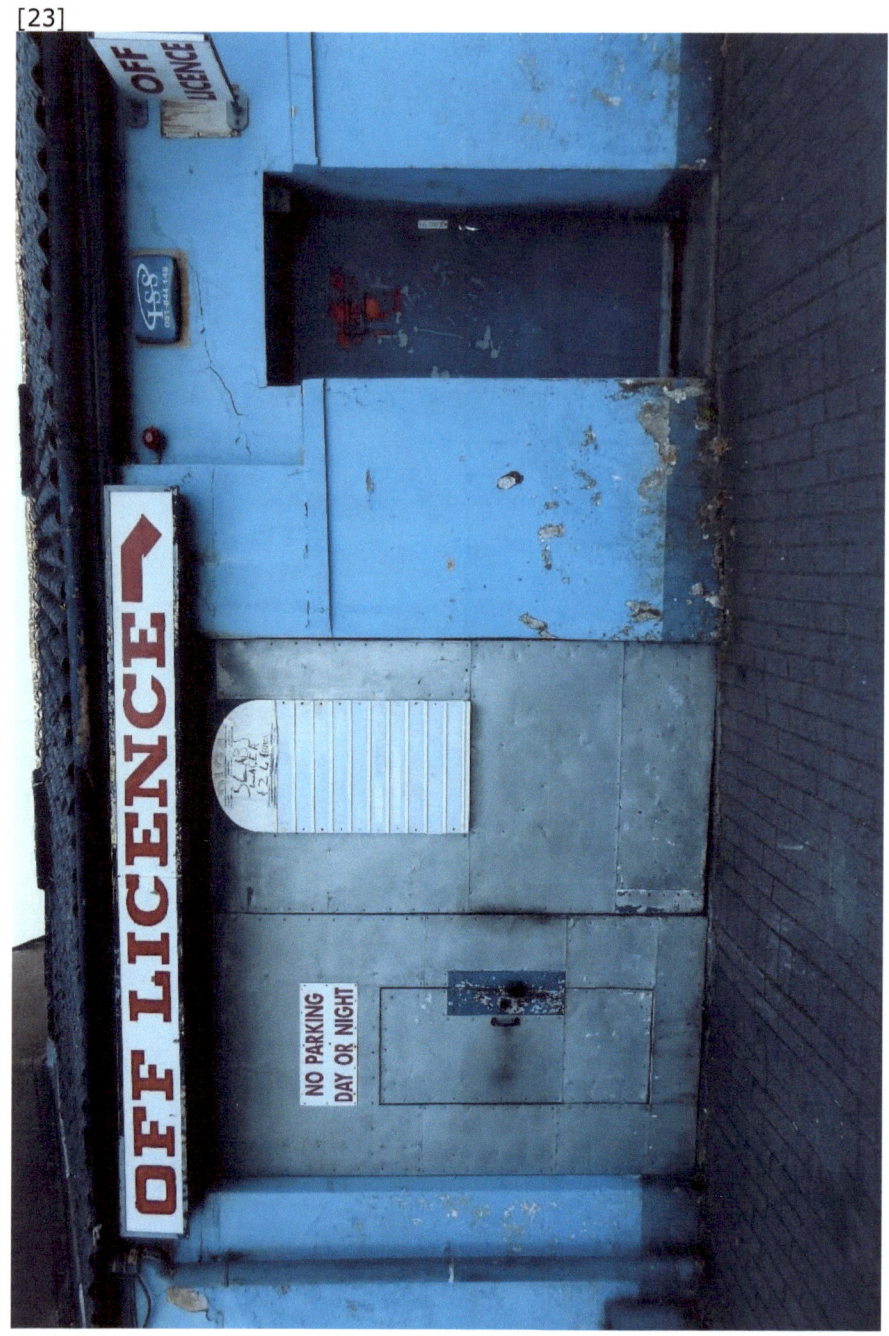

[24]

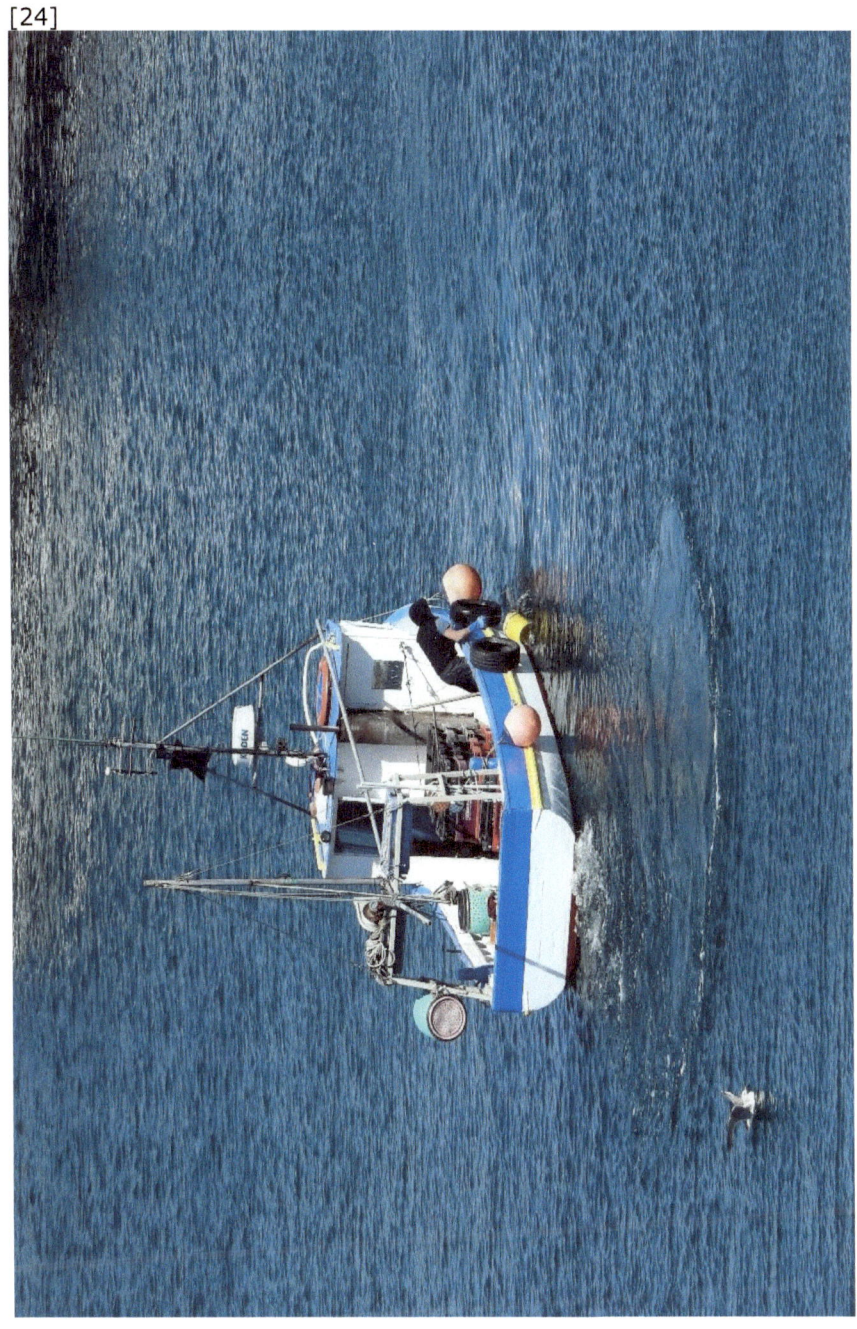

[25]
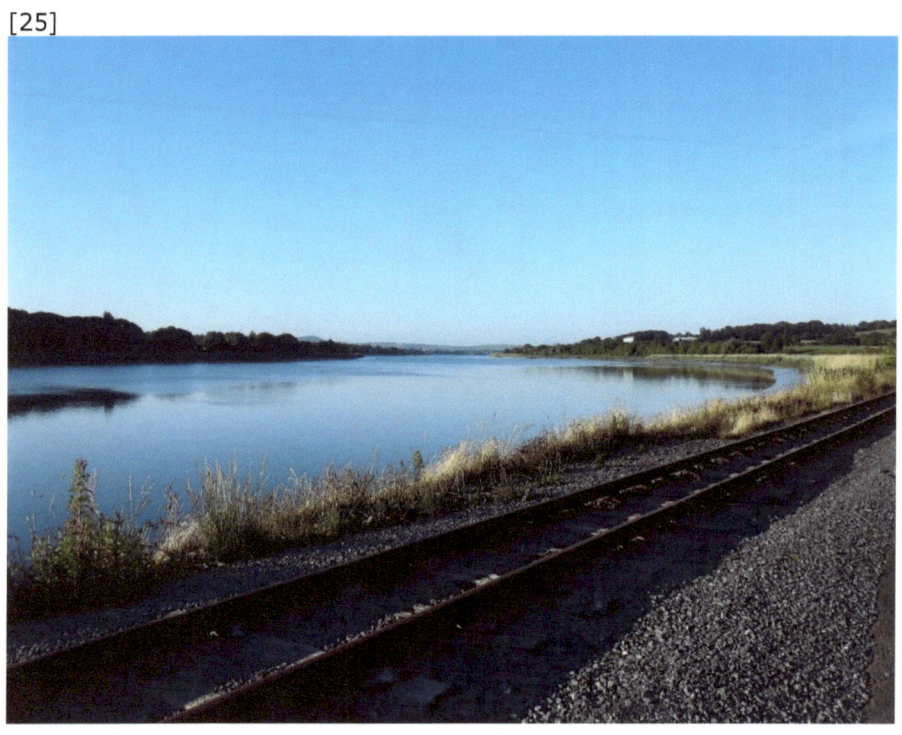

[26]

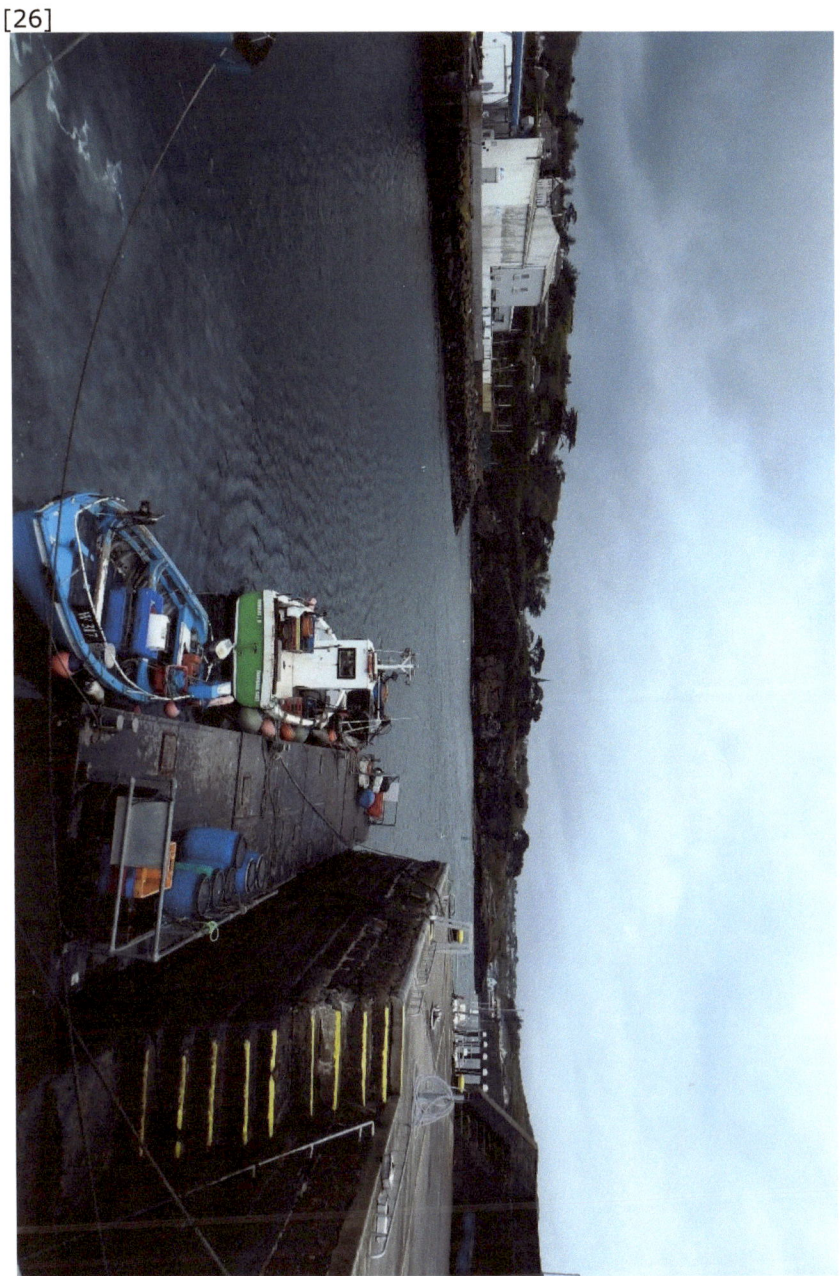

[27]
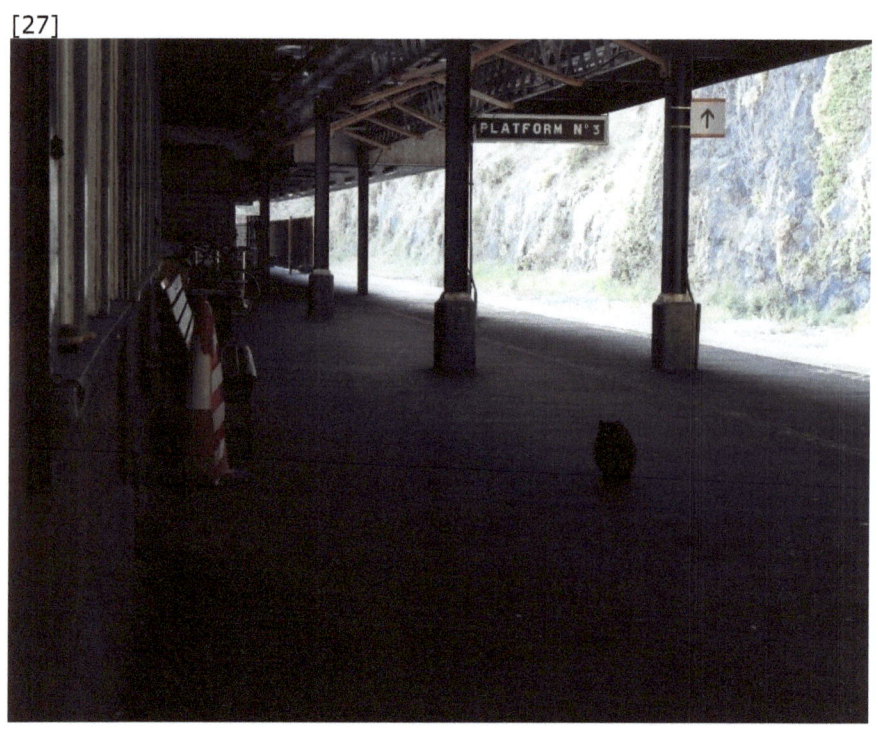

[28]
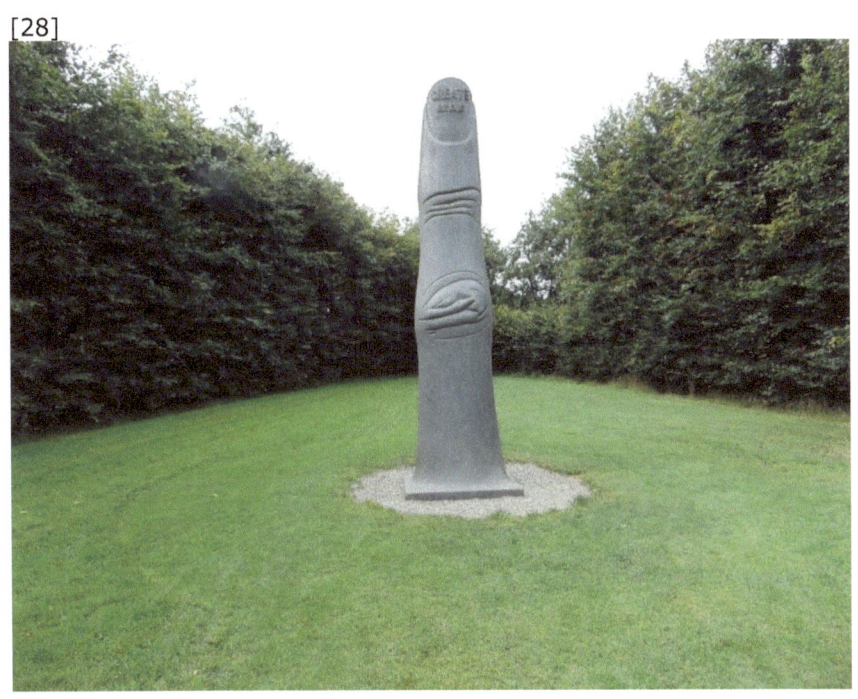

[29]

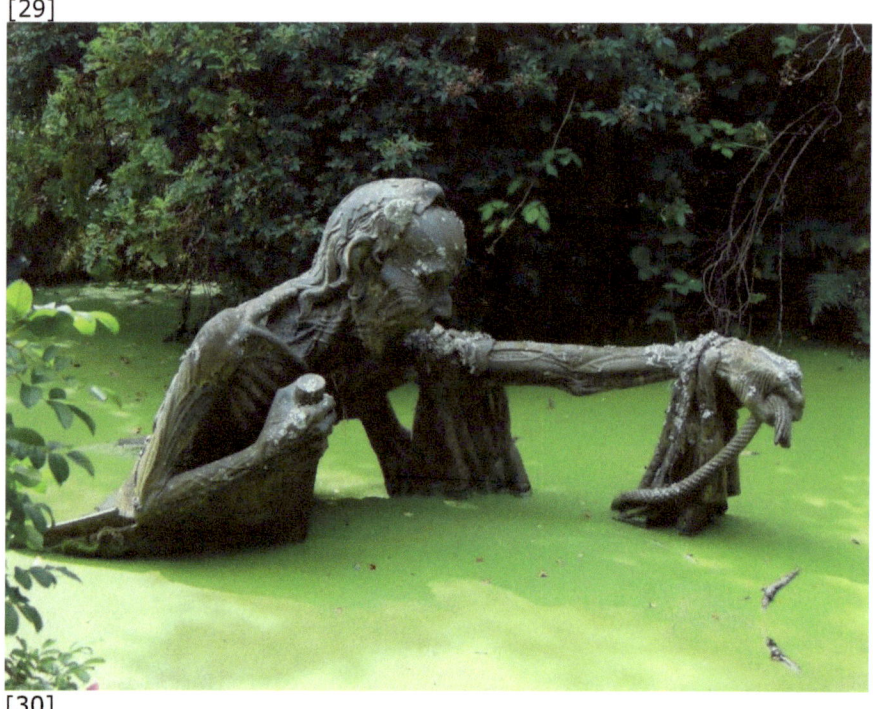

[30]

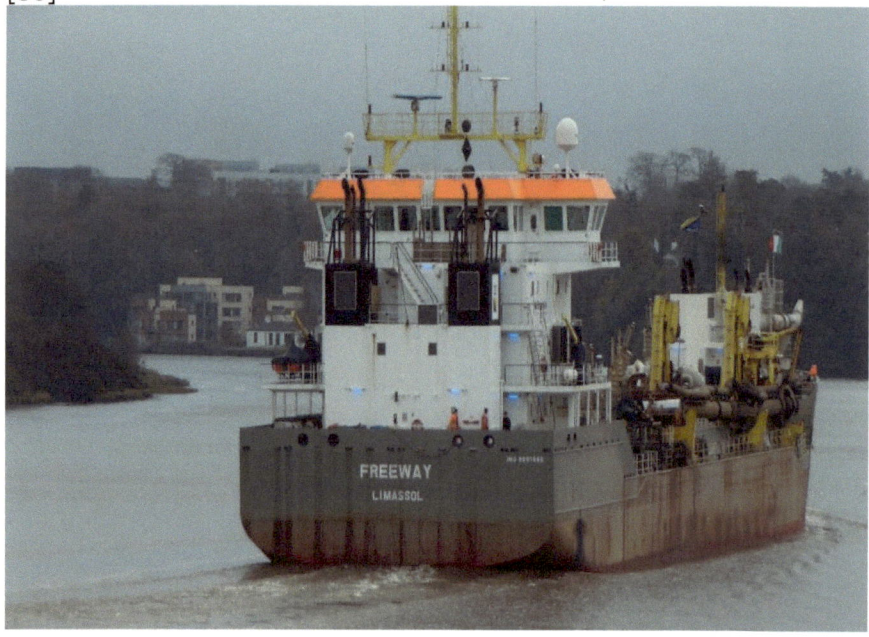

[31]

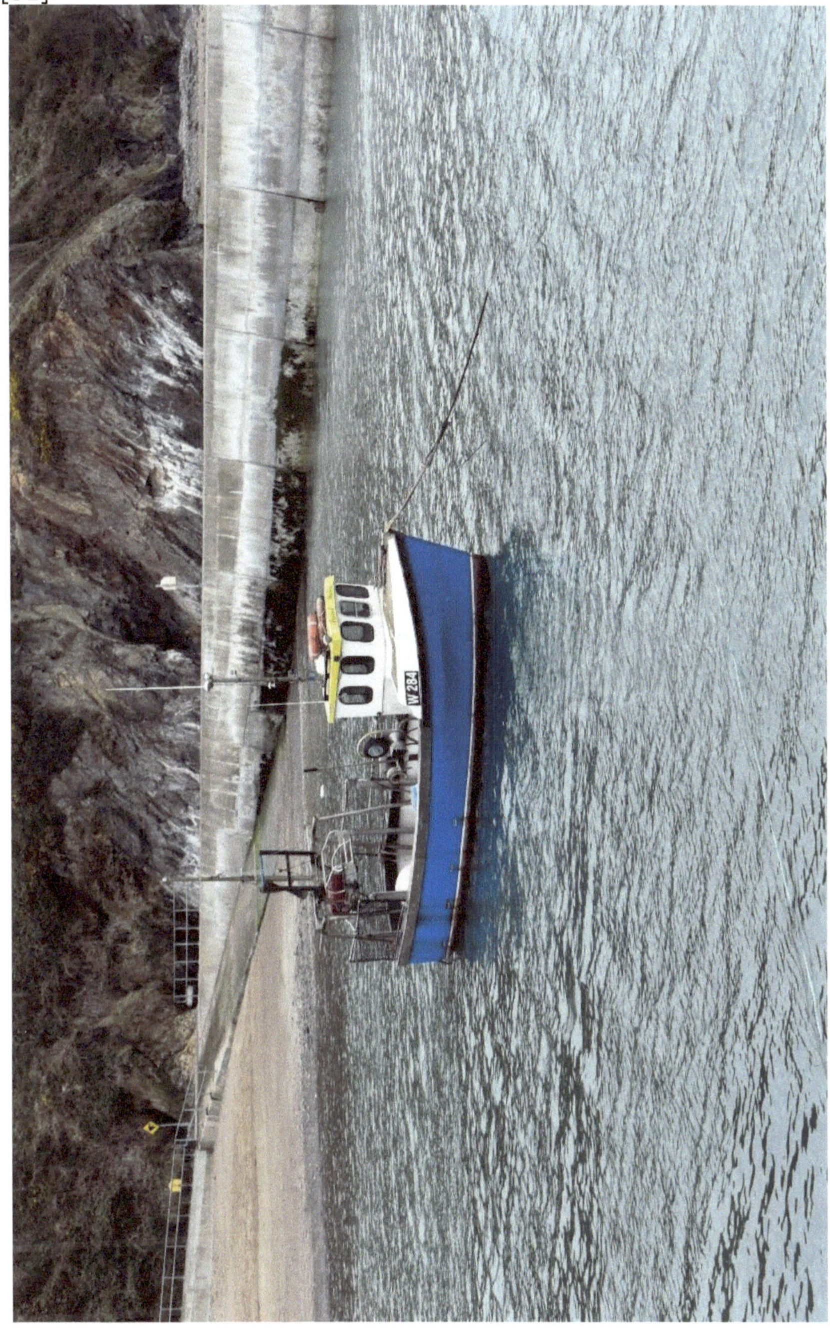

[32]

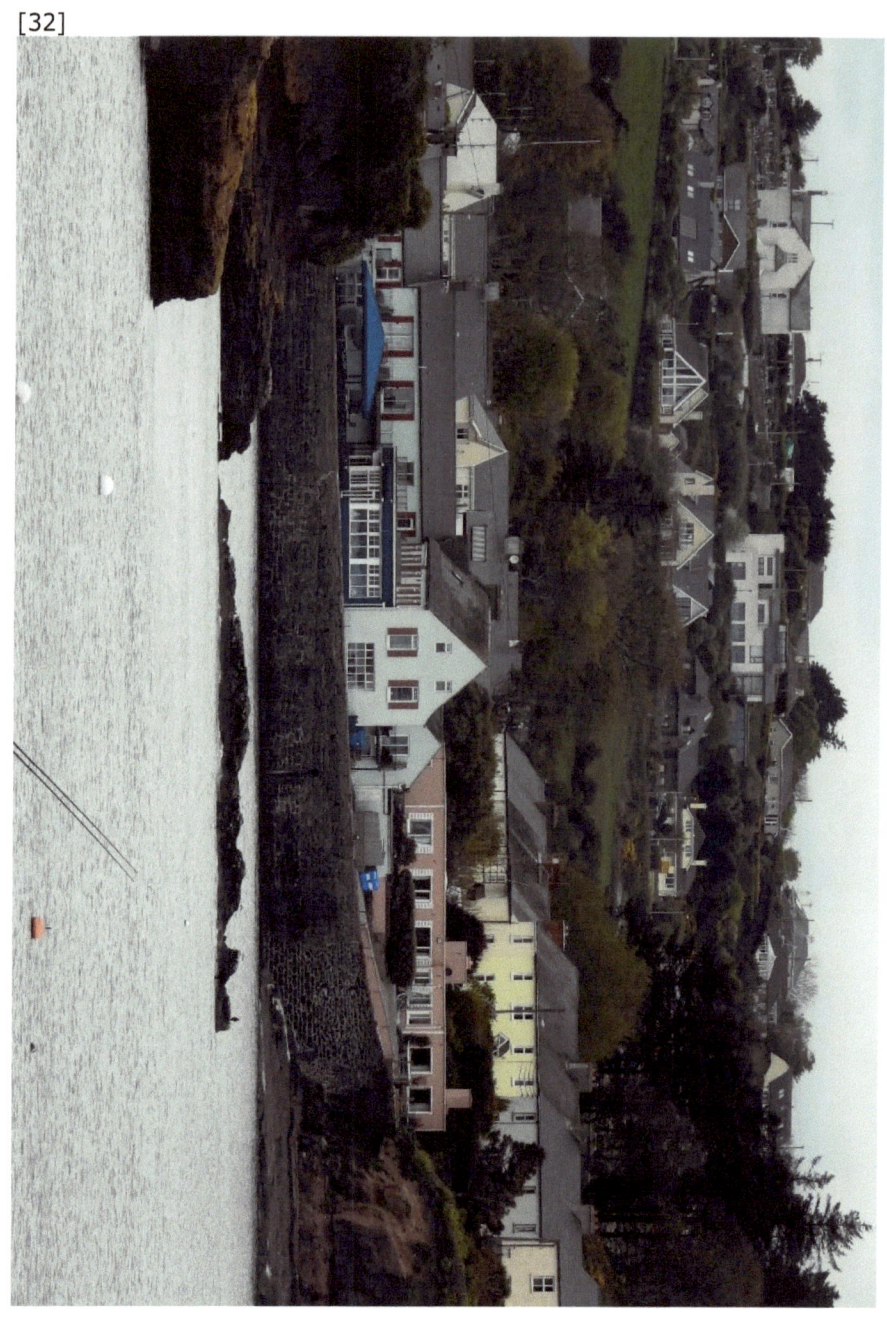

[33]

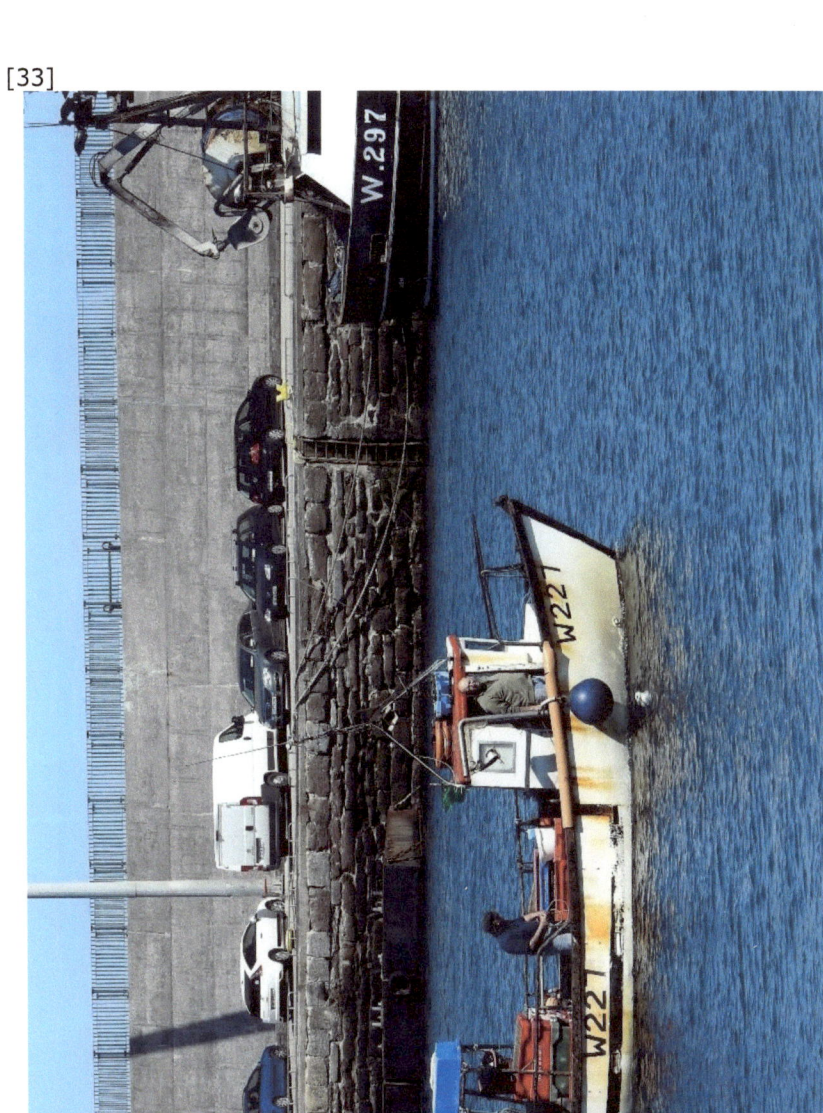

[34]

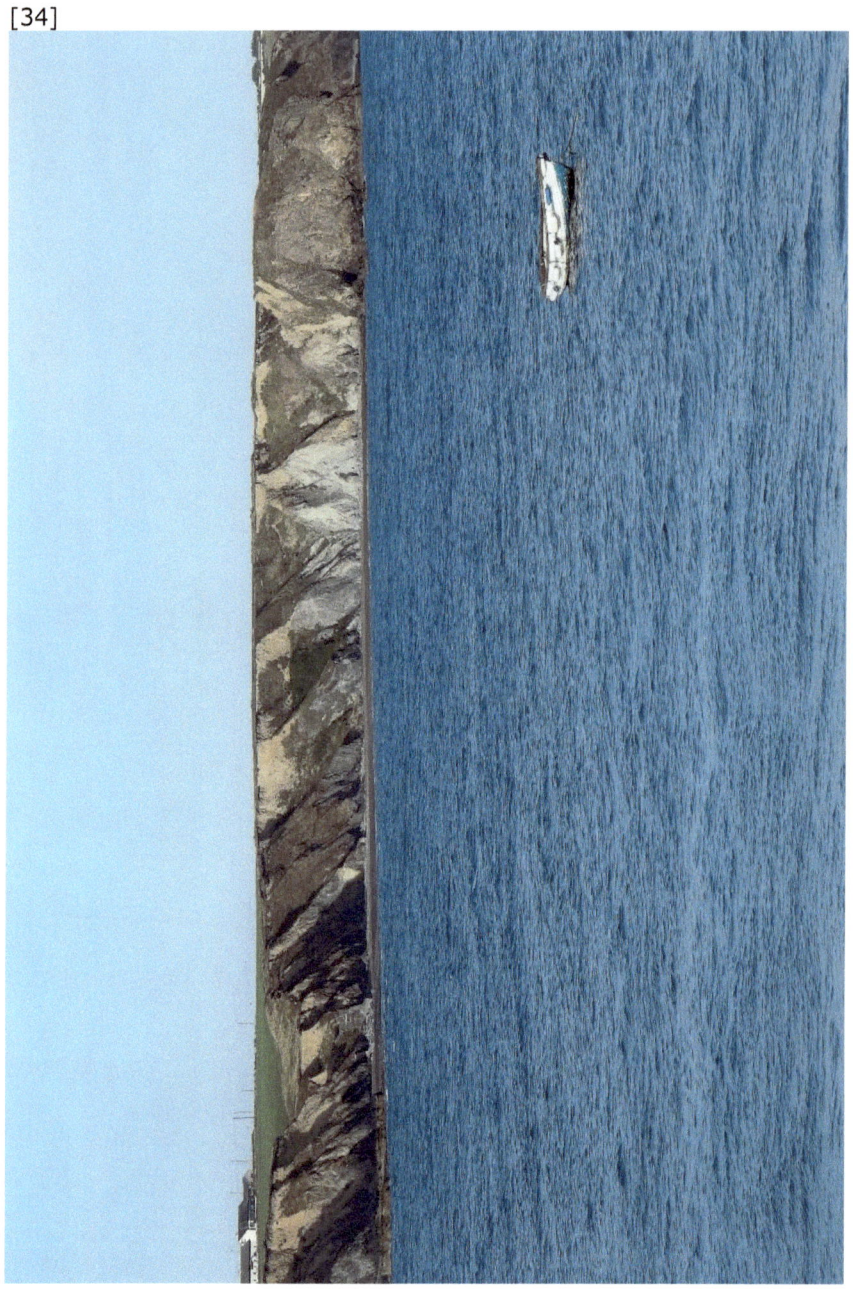

[35]

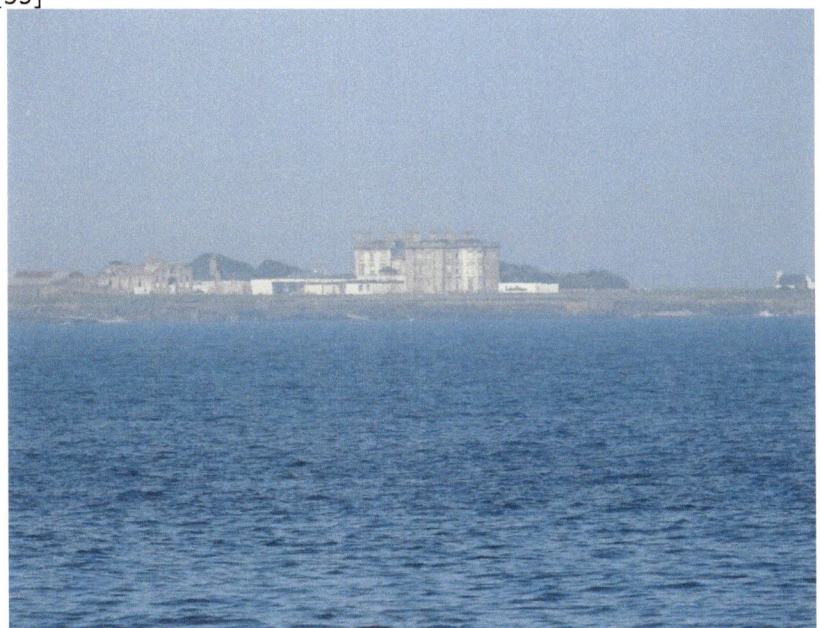

[36]

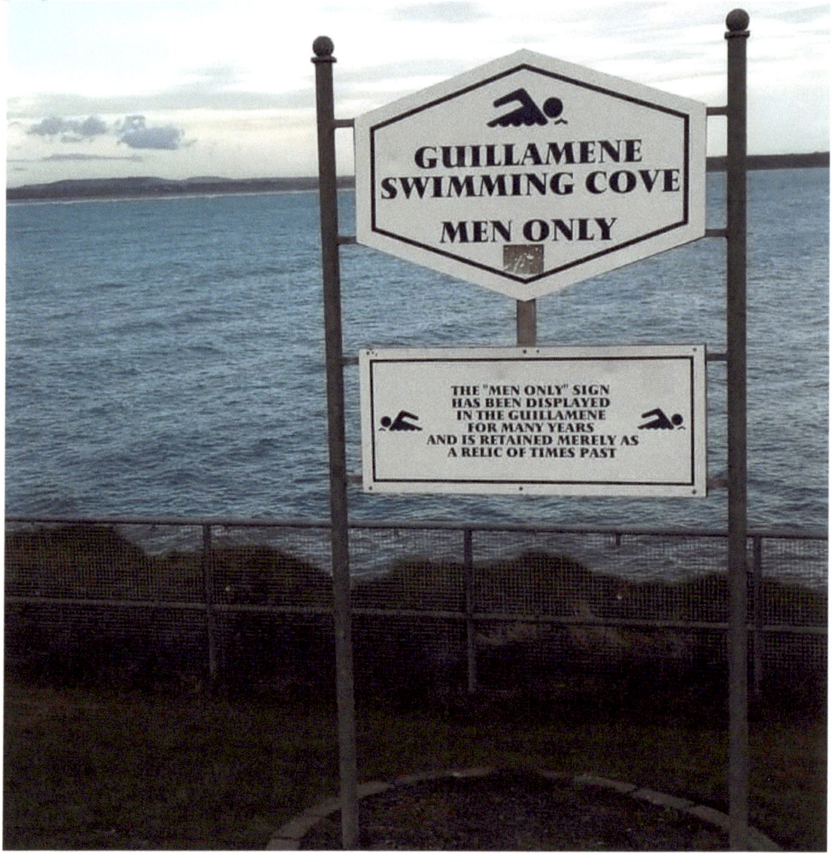

[37]

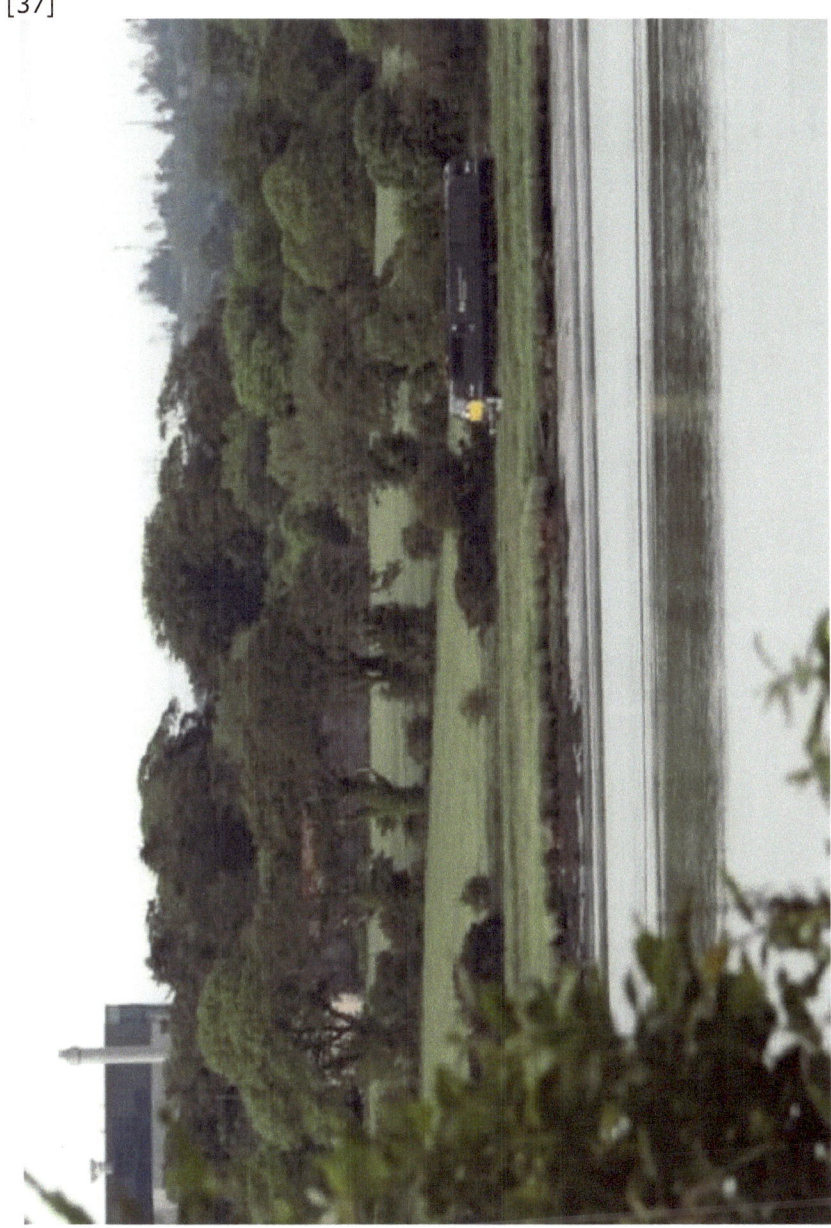

[38]

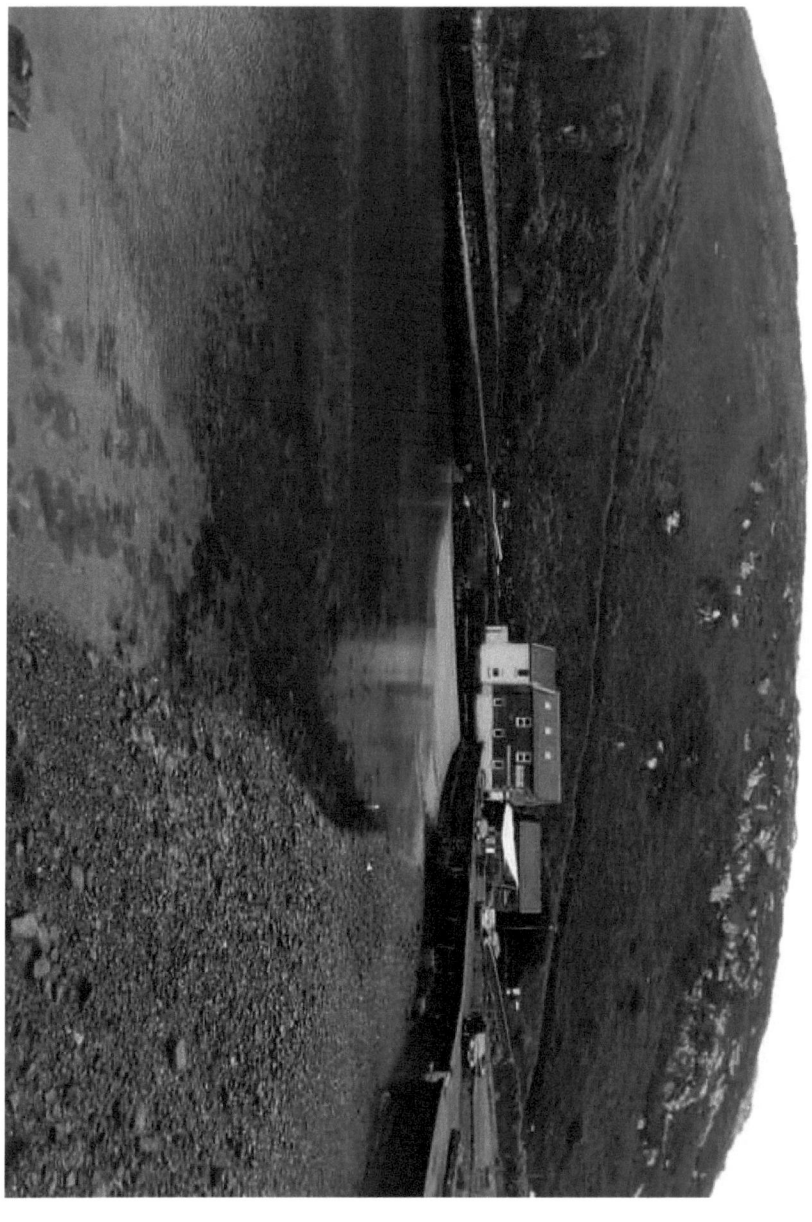

[39]

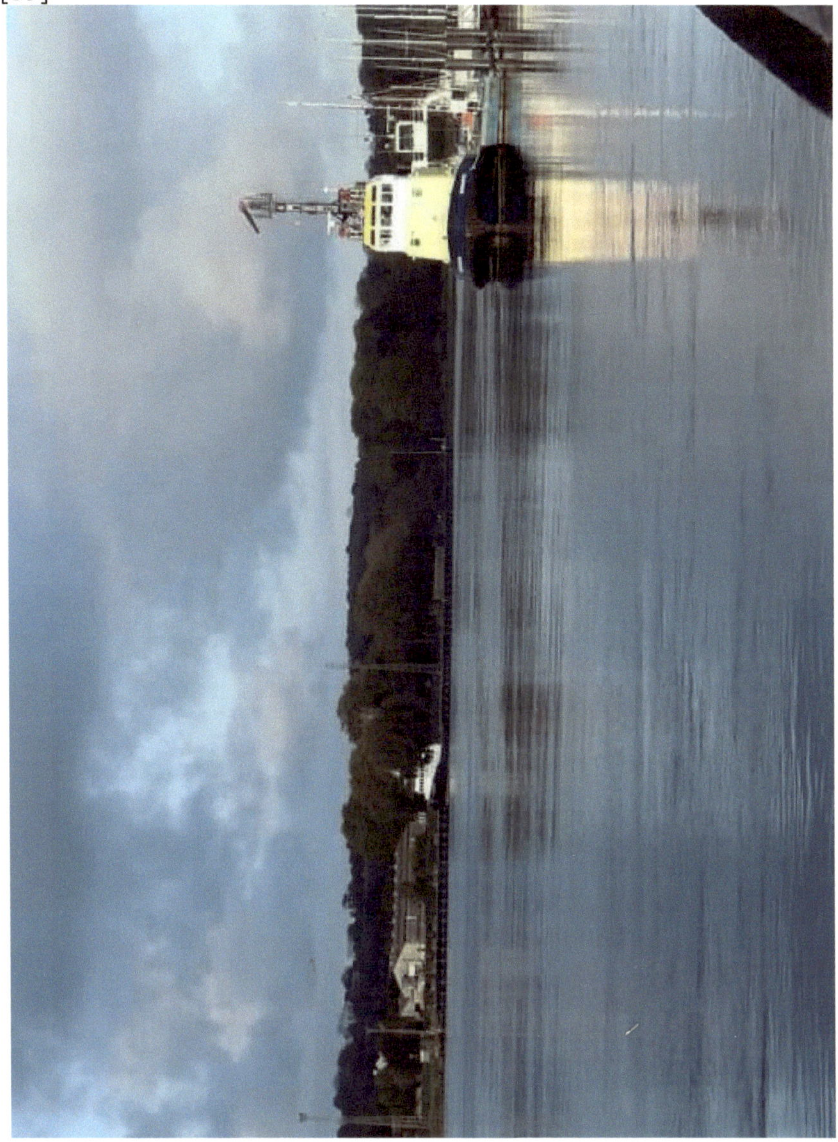

[40]

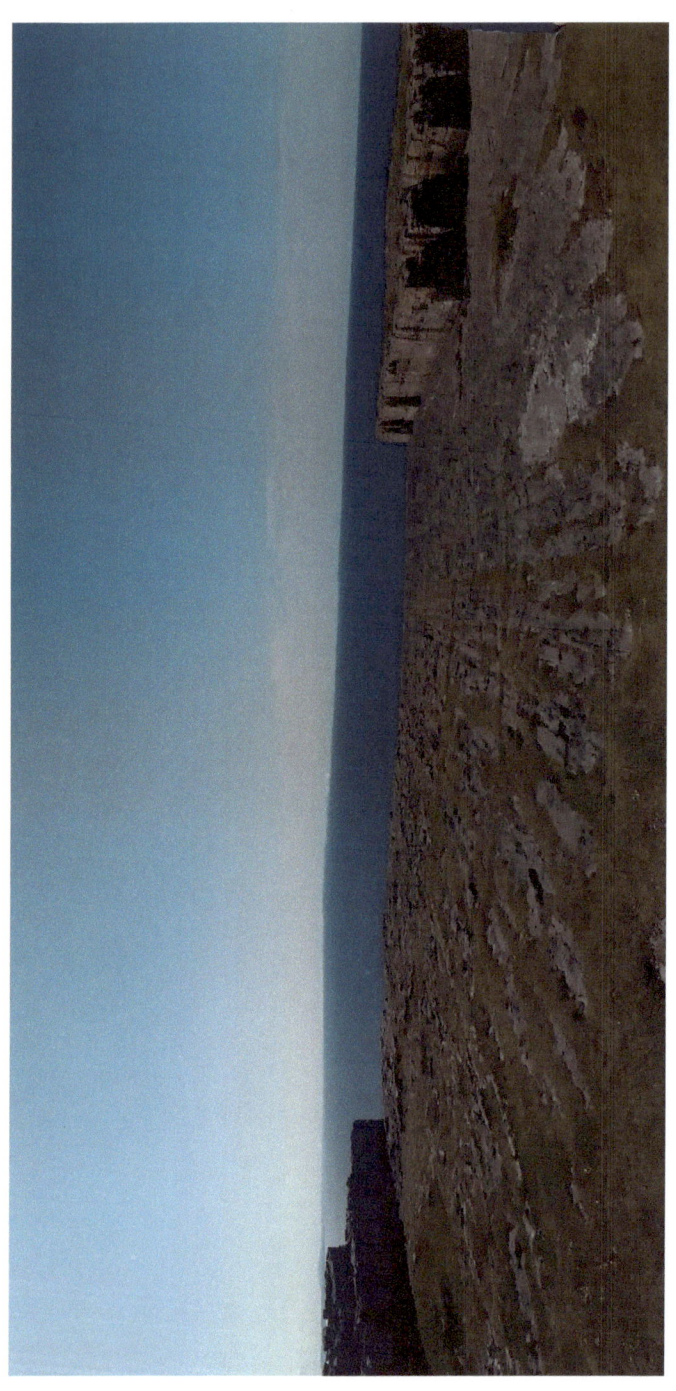

[41]

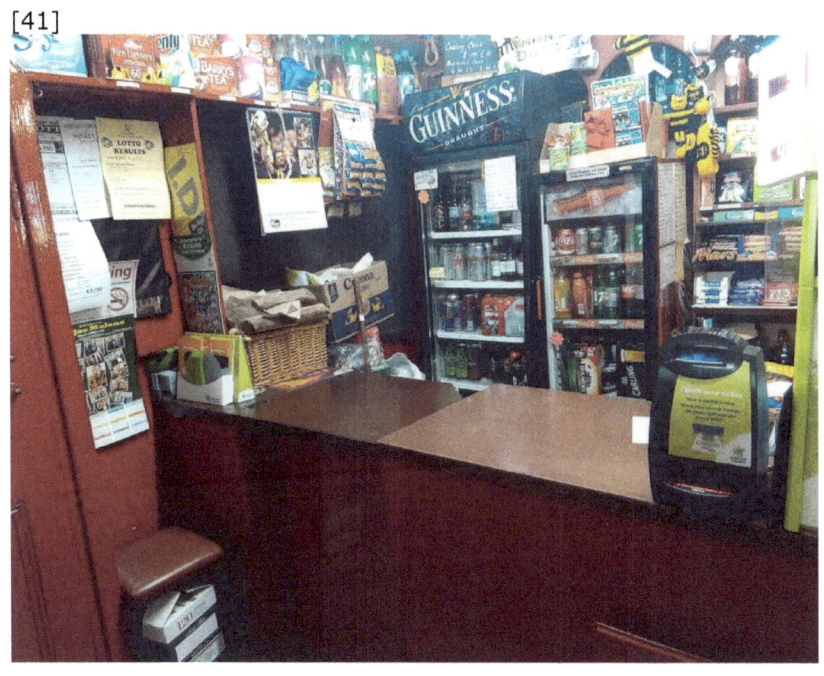

[42]

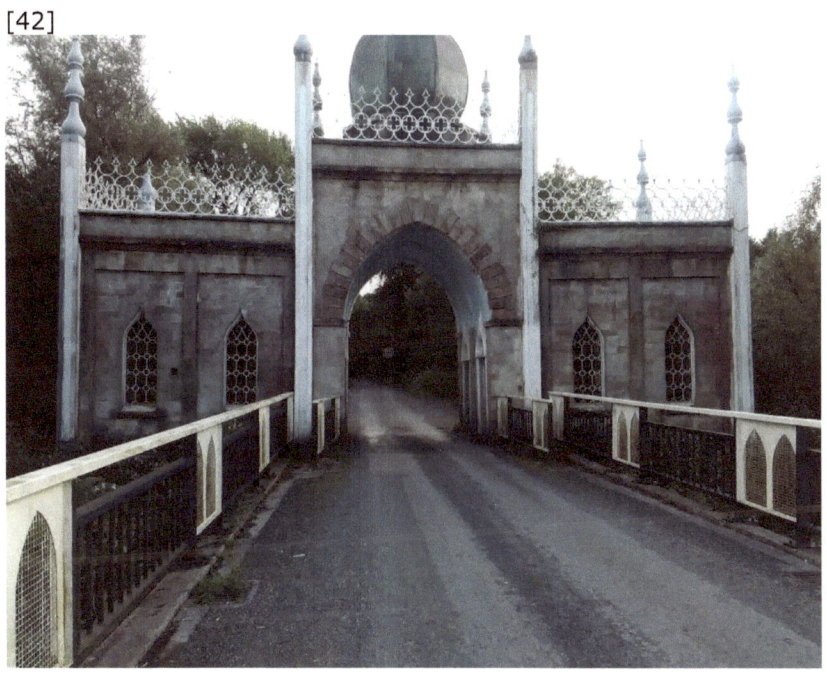

[43]

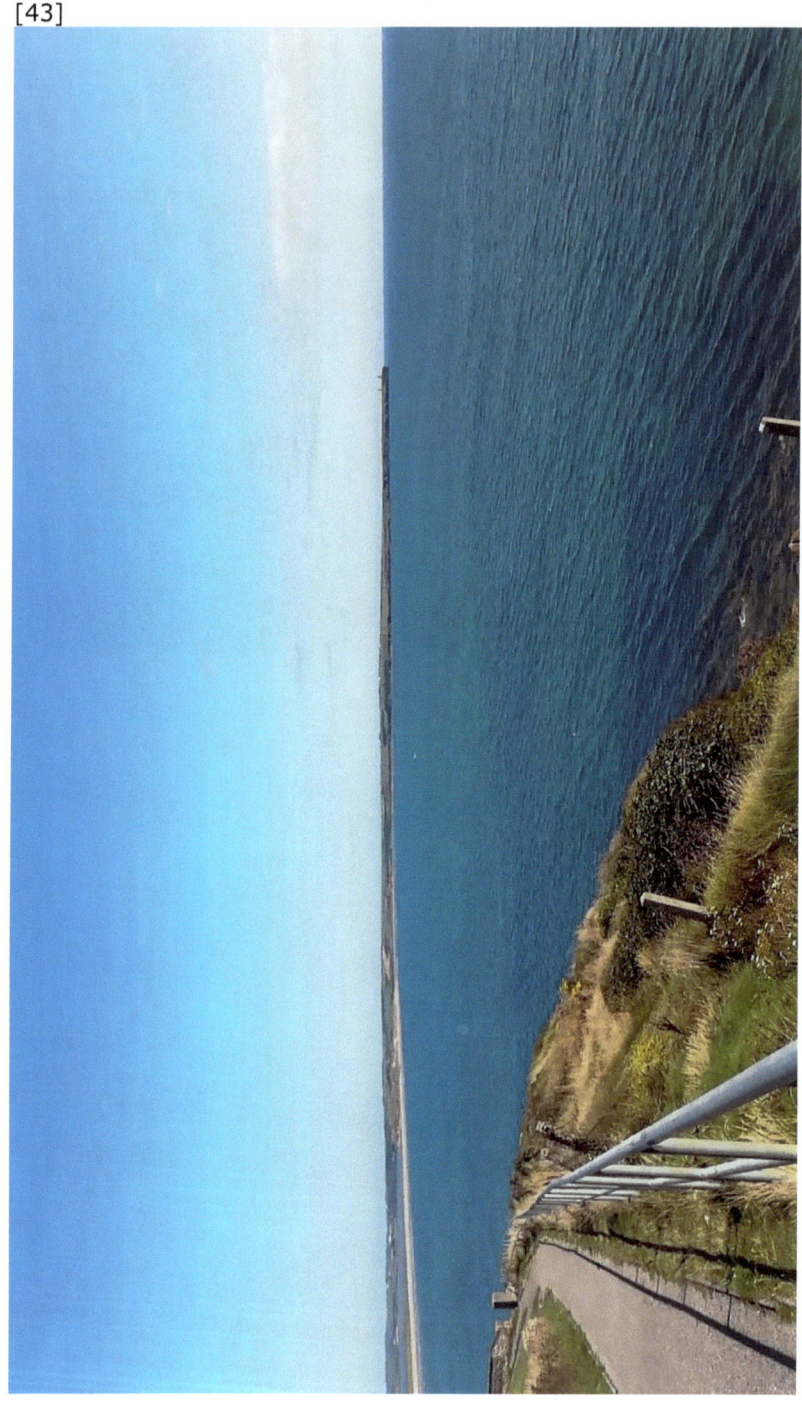

www.ingramcontent.com/pod-product-compliance
Lightning Source LLC
Chambersburg PA
CBHW040336220526
45473CB00009B/2700